Cambridge Elements

Elements in the Philosophy of Georg Wilhelm Friedrich Hegel
edited by
Sebastian Stein
Heidelberg University
Joshua Wretzel
Pennsylvania State University

HEGEL ON THE FAMILY FORM

Andreja Novakovic
University of California, Berkeley

CAMBRIDGE
UNIVERSITY PRESS

Shaftesbury Road, Cambridge CB2 8EA, United Kingdom

One Liberty Plaza, 20th Floor, New York, NY 10006, USA

477 Williamstown Road, Port Melbourne, VIC 3207, Australia

314–321, 3rd Floor, Plot 3, Splendor Forum, Jasola District Centre, New Delhi – 110025, India

Cambridge University Press is part of Cambridge University Press & Assessment, a department of the University of Cambridge.

We share the University's mission to contribute to society through the pursuit of education, learning and research at the highest international levels of excellence.

www.cambridge.org
Information on this title: www.cambridge.org/9781009586764
DOI: 10.1017/9781009586733

© Andreja Novakovic 2026

This publication is in copyright. Subject to statutory exception and to the provisions of relevant collective licensing agreements, no reproduction of any part may take place without the written permission of Cambridge University Press & Assessment.

When citing this work, please include a reference to the DOI 10.1017/9781009586733

First published 2026

A catalogue record for this publication is available from the British Library

ISBN 978-1-009-58676-4 Hardback
ISBN 978-1-009-58671-9 Paperback
ISSN 2976-5684 (online)
ISSN 2976-5676 (print)

Cambridge University Press & Assessment has no responsibility for the persistence or accuracy of URLs for external or third-party internet websites referred to in this publication and does not guarantee that any content on such websites is, or will remain, accurate or appropriate.

For EU product safety concerns, contact us at Calle de José Abascal, 56, 1°, 28003 Madrid, Spain, or email eugpsr@cambridge.org

Hegel on the Family Form

Elements in the Philosophy of Georg Wilhelm Friedrich Hegel

DOI: 10.1017/9781009586733
First published online: January 2026

Andreja Novakovic
University of California, Berkeley

Author for correspondence: Andreja Novakovic, andreja@berkeley.edu

Abstract: Hegel famously argues that the patriarchal, bourgeois nuclear family is a rational institution worth defending. Scholars have asked what exactly to do with this seemingly outdated part of his social and political philosophy. In particular, they have wondered whether Hegel's concept of the family can accommodate changes to our understanding of what counts as a family and what constitutes family relations. In this Element, I ask whether Hegel's defense of the family can be reconciled with family abolition, the project not of reforming the family as an institution, but of radically transforming it beyond recognition. By examining the three relationships that Hegel associates with the family – brothers and sisters, husbands and wives, and parents and children – I argue that Hegel's concept of the family can be reconciled with family abolition so described. What Hegel provides is an account of the family as a site at which important goods have been discovered and developed, without claiming that the family as an institution is necessary for, or even ideally suited to, their continued realization. These goods are singular individuality, ethical love, and material resources.

Keywords: Hegel, feminism, family, marriage, gender

© Andreja Novakovic 2026

ISBNs: 9781009586764 (HB), 9781009586719 (PB), 9781009586733 (OC)
ISSNs: 2976-5684 (online), 2976-5676 (print)

Contents

1 Introduction 1

2 Brothers and Sisters 14

3 Husbands and Wives 27

4 Parents and Children 42

5 Conclusion 56

Bibliography 58

1 Introduction

"The world is constantly evolving, while the family endeavors to stay the same. Updated, refurbished, modernized, but essentially the same. A house in the landscape, both shelter and prison."

-Rachel Cusk, *Aftermath*

Reform or Abolition

This Element will be about Hegel's concept of the family. Before I turn to this topic, a few words about the family today. The family is a controversial institution. There are many for whom it represents an invaluable and indispensable sanctuary in human life. Then there are many for whom it leaves much to be desired. The family has often been described as a source of unhappiness that can fill thousand-page novels; of unfreedom that subjects individuals to arbitrary control; of inequality in the form of inherited advantages and disadvantages.[1] Anti-racists have argued that the family has been used as a tool of racist control, forcing people of color to conform to a family ideal all the while ravaging their kinship relations.[2] And feminists have criticized the family for entrenching gender roles and in effect inculcating these roles into the next generation, for not only does the family compel women to shoulder the lion's share of domestic labor, it also teaches children who are closely watching their parents' lives that this is what they can expect from their own.[3] The family as a form of life moreover seems to be without viable alternative, for people who opt out of forming families often face social isolation and alienation. Even though its modern variant is historically contingent, the family has grown so deep-seated that it has become easier to imagine the end of the world than the end of the family.[4]

To be fair, the family is not (or no longer) monolithic, for there has been a proliferation of different forms of family life. With the advent of same-sex marriage, the family has ceased to be an exclusively heterosexual institution. There are also groups of people that found families without being married, monogamous, or related to those they parent. Some families involve the raising

---
[1] Some liberals have objected to the family because it conflicts with equality of opportunity. It is widely known that even Rawls expressed reservations about the family in *Theory of Justice*, p. 301.
[2] See discussions of family relations under slavery in Angela Davis, *Women Race & Class,* and Hortense Spiller, "Mama's Baby, Papa's Maybe."
[3] This can also be framed in terms of justice in the family. See Susan Moller Okin, *Justice, Gender, and the Family.*
[4] I am taking this formulation from Mark Fisher, *Capitalist Realism,* who wrote that "it's easier to imagine the end of the world than the end of capitalism" (p. 1), and from Sophie Lewis, who adds that it might even "be easier to imagine the end of capitalism … than the end of the family" (Sophie Lewis, *Abolish the Family*, p. 6).

of young people, others do not. All of this suggests that there is a case to be made that the family proves to be plastic, capable of innovation and diversification. This raises questions about what exactly constitutes a family and what differentiates a family from other forms of association. But it does show that the concept of the family, however families are ultimately circumscribed, continues its hold. You might even think that this plasticity contributes to the long life that the family enjoys. In Véronique Munoz-Dardé's words, "The family strikes us as an immutable institution *because* it changes constantly ... it is the instability of social understanding of what constitutes a proper family, and proper family relations, which has allowed for the persistence of the family."[5] In this light, we might think that there is no reason to bother trying to imagine the end of the family. Maybe we should instead continue to reform the family, rather than look for other options.

That said, there has been a newfound interest in a tradition known as *family abolition*, which spans across figures such as Charles Fourier, Alexandra Kollontai, and Shulamith Firestone and today Sophie Lewis and M. E. O'Brien. Although they have different proposals for abolishing the family, they are united in their criticism of the family as such. This tradition's guiding idea is that there is something about the family as a *form* that makes it objectionable in spite of the many mutations that families are undeniably undergoing. No matter how much families change, there are features of the family that remain constant, features that belong to the family as a concept. Here I want to highlight two before explaining what makes them objectionable. The first feature of the family form is that the family is expected to be the primary source of care for its members. This care is both emotional and material: We expect our family members to help us when we are, say, sick, but also to supply a sense of connection and belonging. This is true for adults, but it is especially true for children, who depend on their families for the satisfaction of virtually all of their needs. It is because families provide care that many people continue to be attached to them, both in practice and in theory.[6]

The second feature is that the family hinges on "a boundary between outside and inside" (to borrow M. E. O'Brien's words).[7] This seems to be an especially pronounced feature of modern nuclear families, which have separated themselves from wider kinship relations, although we might think that it applies to

---

[5] Véronique Munoz-Dardé, "Is the Family to be Abolished Then?" p. 55.
[6] In *Minimizing Marriage*, Elizabeth Brake argues that care is a "minimal good" that needs to be ensured by the state. She concludes that this means that the state should protect any relationship that provides such care, whether or not it conforms to the concept of marriage (and presumably also of the family).
[7] O'Brien, *Family Abolition*, p. 40.

a limited extent to extended families as well. The family form is the family as nucleus, as self-enclosed unit, a "monad" of sorts. I think we can accept that this is true of the family form, even as families change shape and cease to be identified with the heterosexual, two-parent household. The point is that families are only intelligible in virtue of a clear-cut distinction between those who are their members and those who are not. The way that the tradition of family abolition captures this idea is by saying that families are private, and hence presuppose a separation between what is private and what is public. If you combine these two features of the family form, you arrive at a conception of families as *privatized sources of care*. The tradition of family abolition holds that this combination makes the family form objectionable. Because families are so meager and yet saddled with a task so vast, they can be described as an "organized poverty" (to borrow Sophie Lewis' phrase).[8] This would be a criticism of families on their own terms, suggesting that families are ill-equipped to deliver that which they promise. Why wouldn't we want to find out whether a greater abundance is possible for us?

There is a lot that stands in the way. One problem is that concrete proposals for abolishing the family tend to strike people as utopian, and they often deliberately are. Although the tradition of family abolition is inspired by real examples that have pointed beyond the family – Israeli kibbutzim, collective households during times of protest – it is also clear that most of these proposals are yet to be put into practice. Furthermore, it has been argued that family abolition cannot happen in isolation from other social changes, making it only one element in a broader revolutionary struggle. If we try to abolish the family while leaving everything else intact, experiments in family abolition cannot be sustained. Another problem lies in the fact that family abolition sounds dystopic, calling to mind images of children being separated from parents and forced into state-run institutions – images that have their basis in reality. We might worry that without the family, all we would have left is the state, an institution even less well suited to satisfying our need for care, especially of the emotional variety. But the figures in this tradition have not tended to argue in favor of state-run institutions – even of "well-run orphanages" – as some people have feared.[9] They are interested in developing alternatives to the family, other ways of organizing our emotional and material lives, rather than eliminating families and relegating individuals to whatever is left standing in their wake.

Recent revivals of family abolition have stressed that the project of abolishing the family should not be understood only negatively, i.e. as an effort to

---

[8] Lewis, *Abolish the family*, p. 4.
[9] See Munoz-Dardé, "Is the Family to be Abolished Then?" especially her discussion of Russell, pp. 48–49.

do away with whatever is currently in place. This makes it different from that of abolishing prisons, or abolishing slavery. Family abolition is instead the call to a radical transformation of the family as we know it. Both Sophie Lewis and M. E. O'Brien have appealed to Hegel, suggesting that abolition is best understood in terms of Hegel's notion of *Aufhebung*. Although they are not invoking Hegel's narrowly technical use of this term, what makes *Aufhebung* so fruitful for them is that the term encompasses seemingly incompatible meanings, which has the advantage of capturing family abolition's wide range of aspirations. *Aufhebung* is a simultaneous "destruction-preservation-transformation-realization."[10] In the context of family abolition this means that *Aufhebung* is a "preserving what is crucial to [the family] – human love, connection, care, community, romance – without binding these qualities to the particular form of the household within capitalism."[11] So, family abolitionists are not recommending, as Sophie K. Rosa puts it, "throwing the baby out with the bathwater."[12] Rather, they suggest that there might be far better ways of achieving these valuable goods that the family promises to deliver.

Hegel's notion of *Aufhebung* can direct thinking about radical transformation in a limited sense. Although Hegel has a narrow understanding of *Aufhebung*, according to which it refers to a dialectical process that can only be retrospectively identified as such, a broader understanding of *Aufhebung* suggests that these seemingly incompatible meanings can be incorporated into one project while leaving room for the emergence of something genuinely new, something we cannot yet clearly discern. The key here is that *Aufhebung* in a loosely Hegelian sense is a radical transformation from one concept to another where the new concept preserves and integrates crucial elements from the former. With the help of *Aufhebung*, it is possible to be critical of the family form on its own terms and be convinced that it needs to be overcome, without needing to be in a position to articulate a better alternative or offer a blueprint for what is to take its place. And with the help of *Aufhebung*, it is possible to work toward radical transformation while remaining curious to find out what comes next. But Hegel is an admittedly unlikely ally. According to a familiar story, the young Hegel was excited by the explosive potential of revolutionary change, whereas the old Hegel grew risk-averse, reluctant to challenge institutional structures or entertain the possibility that change might require avenues not yet made available by

---

[10] Lewis, *Abolish the Family*, p. 81. [11] O'Brien, *Family Abolition*, p. 56.

[12] Rosa, *Radical Intimacy*, p. 96. Her target is specifically the nuclear family. She also writes that this project "asks for the flourishing of all the things that the nuclear family promises but does not deliver: cradling kinship for everyone, characterized by loving commitment, safety, care, and camaraderie" (p. 94).

the social order of his time. In Seyla Benhabib's resounding words, "Hegel saw the future, and he did not like it."[13]

Realizing Freedom

This is especially striking in the case of Hegel's views about the family. In his *Elements of the Philosophy of Right*, Hegel devotes the first part of his chapter on ethical life to the family, designating it as one of the three central spheres (alongside civil society and the state) integral to a rational social order. For Hegel, it is crucial that the family be a sphere distinct from civil society and the state, even though they can only accomplish their functions through cooperation. Hegel clearly wants to defend the family as such a distinct sphere, which is why he devotes an entire chapter to it. The fact that Hegel addresses the family at all is a virtue of his political philosophy, for this alone places him on a rather short list of figures who took the family seriously, rather than taking it for granted as a background institution that is either an ineradicable fixture of human life or obviously necessary for the development of citizens.[14] Although the family as an institution already exists and has existed for a long time, Hegel thinks that the family nevertheless needs to be first determined and evaluated.

As I mentioned, the family is usually said to be in the service of satisfying our needs, primarily our need for care. It would have been open to Hegel to take a similar route, for he could have proceeded from the fact that the human species has to reproduce itself, or the fact that children demand long term caregiving, and then argue that the family fulfills these natural functions, functions that would need to be fulfilled anywhere and anytime. Without denying these facts about us as biological creatures, Hegel adopts a different strategy. His starting point is not the satisfaction of natural needs, but the realization of freedom, which is a historically emergent ideal. So it is freedom that provides Hegel with the basis on which the family is to be determined and evaluated. Since "freedom" is not usually the first term that comes to mind in connection with the family, it makes his position intriguingly counterintuitive. Of course, Hegel is not committed to a narrowly liberal conception of freedom. To provide a preview, freedom is for Hegel a relational concept, a "being by oneself in

---

[13] Benhabib, "On Hegel, Women and Irony," p. 254. Benhabib has in mind free-spirited women among Hegel's acquaintances. Given that such women were exceptions to a widespread rule, I doubt that Hegel would have (or could have) seen these women as evidence of a future whose arrival he wanted to halt.

[14] Okin points this out in *Justice, Gender, and the Family*. She criticizes contemporary political philosophers for ignoring the family and mentions Hegel among other historical figures who did write about the family (pp. 18 – 19).

another."[15] As we will see in greater detail, Hegel argues that freedom in this relational sense is a social achievement that requires standing in determinate relations of recognition with others.[16]

Hegel defends the family because he believes that it represents a domain in which freedom in this relational sense is realized. Since the same can be said of the other two social spheres, the family must be distinguished from civil society and from the state in terms of what in another person is being recognized and how it is being recognized. It would be helpful to take a cursory look at how Hegel defines the family in broad strokes:

> The family, as the immediate substantiality of spirit, has as its determination the spirit's feeling of its own unity, which is love. Thus, the disposition [appropriate to the family] is to have self-consciousness of one's individuality within this unity as essentiality which has being in and for itself, so that one is present in it not as an independent person but as a member. (PR ¶158)

Hegel is here characterizing the family as a sphere of individuality, a sphere in which individuality can flourish, though what exactly this means will need to be spelled out. To put this in terms of freedom, Hegel is suggesting that the family provides ongoing relations in which individuals are recognized as individuals by one another. It is because recognizing individuality will require intimacy and nurture that Hegel conceives of the family in terms of love, and by implication in terms of care. But the care in question cannot be directed only at our neediness as members of the human species. Rather, care in all its different forms must be guided by the demands of reciprocal recognition, so by the demands of realizing freedom.

So far, I have provided Hegel's broad account of the family and his general approach to defending it. But Hegel goes well beyond defending the family as such, for he goes on to defend a highly specific version of it. In the *Philosophy of Right*, Hegel describes the family in a way that bears an undeniable resemblance to the family in his time and place. For example, Hegel emphasizes that the modern family is nuclear, having separated itself from broader kinship relations [*Stämme*].[17] According to Hegel, the family is paradigmatically a husband and a wife who become a single person through marriage and who have a child that is born from their union. Hegel proceeds to describe the couple in terms of gender

---

[15] It is sometimes translated, "being *at home* in another," which already stacks the cards in the family's favor.

[16] See Frederick Neuhouser on "social freedom" in the *Foundations of Hegel's Social Theory*.

[17] Hegel makes this point in PR §172. See Susanne Lettow, "Re-articulating Genealogy: Hegel on Kinship, Race and Reproduction" for a discussion of Hegel's general views about kinship relations and how these views interact with both his account of the family and his accounts of racial and sexual differences.

specific role obligations: the husband is tasked with procuring resources and managing these resources as the family's head, while the wife fulfills her "vocation" by maintaining the family as a harmonious unity. Hegel is painting a picture of traditional gender roles, even though these gender roles had emerged relatively recently and so would not have been as traditional to him as they seem to us.[18] He is describing a distinctly modern ideal that has emerged as a result of a historical process in which freedom became the overarching norm; and a distinctly bourgeois ideal that does not pertain to the peasant family or the working-class family, where such gender roles were not as sedimented. The underlying implication of his argument is that the modern bourgeois family is especially well suited to the realization of freedom. Since Hegel was himself the member of such a modern bourgeois family, it would have been a welcome conclusion.

It bears emphasizing that Hegel is not presenting this description of the family neutrally. To put it in Alison Stone's words, Hegel is offering a "normative redescription of that emerging division [of gender roles], a redescription in which this division and the family structure bound up with it form essential aspects of reason's progressive self-actualization in the modern social world."[19] This has led to the worry that, as Carole Pateman states, "Hegel's arguments are fatally compromised by his acceptance of the sexual contract," in other words, by what she describes as the erasure of women as independent persons within the marital union.[20] Although Hegel's account of the family remains a relatively neglected part of his *Philosophy of Right*, those scholars who have engaged with it have raised a host of questions about how exactly to deal with Hegel's normative redescription. Are Hegel's claims simply an expression of his sexist prejudices, and if so, do they incriminate his whole project?[21] Or can we dismiss these aspects as antiquated or "quaint" while retaining other aspects that we find less obsolete?[22] Or can we instead charge Hegel with contradicting himself, making claims that conflict with other commitments crucial to his political philosophy (for example, his conception of universal freedom, or his rejection of nature as a basis for social organization)?[23]

---

[18] See Katrin Hausen for her research into the intellectual history of "gender characters."
[19] Stone, "Gender, the Family, and the Organic State," p. 145.
[20] Pateman, *The Sexual Contract*, p. 173.
[21] Stone, "Hegel on law, women, and contract": "Many feminist scholars have argued that these views do not merely reflect Hegel's acceptance of the prejudices of his time, but follow from his legal and political philosophy more broadly, in a way that makes Hegel's entire political philosophy problematic from a feminist viewpoint" (p. 104).
[22] Pinkard, *Hegel's Phenomenology*, p. 304. Allen Wood in *Hegel's Ethical Thought* calls Hegel's views "quaintly repugnant reminders of the social practices of Hegel's age and the prejudices of his class" (p. 243).
[23] For example, Jean-Philippe Deranty, "The 'Son' of Civil Society," argues that Hegel is relying on nature; Joan Landes, "Hegel's Conception of the Family," argues that Hegel's views on women

A related set of interpretive questions revolve around the extent to which Hegel understands the family to be a flexible institution, so whether Hegel's account of the family can accommodate changes that this institution has already undergone and incorporate reforms along the lines that have already unfolded. For example, is Hegel's view compatible with, say, same-sex marriage?[24] Or does his account rise (and thereby fall) with his commitment to the sexual difference between spouses?[25] Even if Hegel was personally opposed to family reform, we might nevertheless wonder whether he is philosophically entitled to his opposition. Hegel was clearly well aware that a lot about the social world he describes in the *Philosophy of Right* is liable to change. However he may have felt about this change, it seems fair to assume that he would not have wanted to construct his account of ethical life in such a way that it is condemned to obsolescence from the start. It is important to my reading of Hegel's method in the *Philosophy of Right* that we be able to distinguish the more fundamental principles to which he is philosophically committed from the concrete institutions in which he believed those principles to be instantiated in his social world.[26] My reading also leaves room for the possibility that the concrete institutions that Hegel describes could be challenged and revised on the basis of these principles, even if Hegel himself does not venture in this direction. Critical approaches to Hegel's *Philosophy of Right*, such as those by Alison Stone and Carole Pateman, among many others, have thus raised important questions by asking us to reconsider whether the family as Hegel understands it can be modified in light of our changing social understandings of what constitutes a proper family or proper family relations.

What they have not yet asked us to consider is whether Hegel's account of the family could extend toward family abolition. At first sight, it seems like this would be going too far. Even if it turns out that the family as Hegel understands it is not as frozen in time as it may appear, it can sound positively outlandish to think that Hegel's overall position could make room for the abolition of the family. First, Hegel takes himself to be offering a defense of the family as a sphere in which freedom is as a matter of fact realized, which seems at odds with the aim of abolishing it. Second, Hegel rejects "moral" (or "moralizing")

---

violate his commitments to civil personality and modern agency; Kimberly Hutchings, *Hegel and Feminist Philosophy*, argues that Hegel's "universal prescriptions" to women are in tension with his commitment to the historical situatedness of all knowledge claims (pp. 106–110).

[24] On this question, see Jim Vernon, "Free-Love," and Philip Kain, "Hegel, Recognition, and Same-Sex Marriage," who argue that there are aspects of Hegel's view that can be harnessed in defense of same-sex marriage.

[25] Edward C. Halper, "Hegel's Family Values," claims that Hegel's "account cannot stand without these differences [in sex roles]" (p. 858).

[26] For more on this reading of Hegel's method, see Novakovic and Maksymchuk, "Hegel and Plato on How to Become Good."

forms of social criticism that demand a utopian alternative to our flawed institutions and that prefer unrealized (and possibly unrealizable) ideals over what is already in place. Third, Hegel sees the family as one element in a broader network of institutions, a pillar in a form of ethical life that Hegel takes to be on the whole worth upholding.[27] Given that the family is interconnected with the other two social spheres, it looks like we could not abolish the family without leaving behind a gaping "functional gap."[28] So, even if we were to accept the more modest (though still controversial) claim that it is consistent with Hegel's project to say that the family for Hegel is flexible enough to allow for its reform, the impression we get is that the family for Hegel could not be flexible enough to allow for its abolition.

Hegel's Family Form

In this Element, I am asking whether this impression is warranted, so whether Hegel's account of the family and family abolition are as irreconcilable as they may seem. Could the family as Hegel understands it become radically transformed as a sphere distinct from the state and civil society, an *Aufhebung* that preserves what is valuable about the family while overcoming its form as a family? We have seen that there is a disagreement between those who want to reform the family but preserve the family form, and those who seek to abolish the family, rather than simply reconfiguring it. Hegel might say that it is not obvious how exactly to draw a stable distinction between internal reform and radical transformation. As Hegel puts on display, even a seemingly local action that raises an initially humble challenge can have revolutionary consequences, undermining not just the family as an autonomous social sphere but also the broader world of which it is a part. What such an action indicates is that the line between internal reform and radical transformation is not hard and fast. But the greater challenge consists in defining the family form once and for all, so that it will be undeniable when we have successfully overcome it and when we have merely reconfigured it. Although Hegel does outline some of the family's characteristic features, he is also alive to the family as a historically evolving concept. If we adhere to Hegel's process of *Aufhebung*, what constitutes a family remains an unsettled question.[29]

---

[27] Hegel describes the family as one 'ethical root of the state' in PR §255.
[28] Neuhouser, *Diagnosing Social Pathologies,* pp. 36–40. Neuhouser argues that each institution is functionally specialized and so depends for its functioning on the existence of other institutions. This places institutional constraints on social transformation. He writes, "Fixing the family requires, at a minimum, reforming civil society" (*Diagnosing Social Pathology*, p. 39).
[29] Axel Honneth in *Freedom's Right* provides a relatively minimal concept of the family inspired broadly by Hegel's *Philosophy of Right*.

With this qualification in mind, I will argue that Hegel does offer ways of thinking about family abolition, even if he is clearly not himself calling for the abolition of the family. We can see how he could be doing one without the other by returning to Hegel's own notion of *Aufhebung*. As I pointed out, the tradition of family abolition acknowledges that there are goods that are central to the family as a concept and that are genuinely valuable, even if this tradition concludes that the family is ill-suited to their achievement. But what are these goods? At first sight we might think that they should be relatively easy to identify, maybe because they are determined by our fundamental human needs: love, care, belonging, etc. The challenge would then consist in determining the optimal way of meeting these needs. What I want to suggest is that Hegel thinks it took a long process of experimenting with the family to discover the goods that the family is to achieve. If we understand this process in terms of *Aufhebung*, we could say we would not have been in a position to determine what these goods are except by experimenting with the family.

Throughout this Element, I will stress that Hegel casts families as *sites of learning*, places where we find out what we need in the first place, or better yet, where we find out how to be free.[30] Even though Hegel is committed to the view that the family has the general task of realizing freedom, knowing this does not yet tell us what exactly it means, namely, which specific goods are within the purview of the family. In the following, I will make a case for the importance of *singular individuality*, *ethical love*, and *material resources*, as specific goods that became first realizable through – and hence first knowable through – participation in family relations. But to learn something at a specific site does not mean to become forever trapped on this site. We can admit that the family allows us to identify these goods that the family is to realize without committing ourselves to the position that these goods can *only* or can *ideally* be realized in the family. Even though Hegel would not have favored the abolition of the family, I do not think that Hegel's account rules out abolishing the family in the sense of radically transforming it, though it does tell us something about the stakes of doing so. We can think of this as placing constraints on the project of family abolition, but also as providing an arsenal of concepts to be used productively in this project, because these concepts specify aspects of the family that are worth keeping in whatever form of life is to take its place.[31]

---

[30] See for example Rahel Jaeggi's conception of forms of life in *Critiques of Form of Life*, and Federica Gregoratto's conception of erotic love in *Love Troubles* as contexts in which learning takes place.

[31] There might be other aspects of Hegel's philosophy, such as his distinct methodology, that could be useful to the project of family abolition, which fall beyond the scope of this Element. Thanks to Livia von Samson for this point.

I will approach Hegel's account of the family by following the path of prior scholars and directing my attention to the family's flexibility as well as its limitations. I am inheriting the following question: If we proceed from Hegel's assumption that the family is an institution that is to realize freedom, which aspects will be without alternative and which aspects can in principle be abandoned? Some scholars have argued that these limitations are stringent, maybe because they think that we cannot cherry-pick our way through the *Philosophy of Right,* leaving behind whatever fails to conform to our intuitions. Others supposed that these limitations are lax, maybe because they assume that the family is ultimately constrained only by the *Science of Logic*, which presents the truly inflexible limitations to which Hegel's project is beholden. On my reading, what Hegel says about the family falls between these two extremes: his account is not tethered to his concrete description of the modern bourgeois family, but it is also not constrained only by the logical concepts outlined elsewhere. The family itself is not a logical concept in Hegel's sense, which means that it cannot be discovered in or deduced from the *Science of Logic*.[32] But the family as a concept is also not developed and revised solely through empirical generalizations about existing families, although it will require attention to the family as an existing institution that has undergone a specific historical development.

Hegel's concept of the family is also often associated with his *Philosophy of Nature*. We need to take seriously the fact that Hegel refers to "nature" whenever he mentions the family, though it is an open question how exactly to interpret these references.[33] The most extreme position would be one that takes Hegel's view of the family to be derivable from his *Philosophy of Nature*. To cite an example, it would mean that Hegel's traditional gender roles can be inferred from his views about biological reproduction. A less extreme position takes natural processes and kinds to be essential to Hegel's concept of the family without fully determining it. According to such a view, the family is the place at which to negotiate the natural side of human life.[34] Hegel indeed emphasizes that the family must *also* provide solutions to problems that stem from our nature as living members of the human species, and it must *also*

---

[32] In this respect I am diverging from Halper in "Hegel's Family Values" who writes, "As far as I can see, Hegel's use of sex roles in his account of the family owns nothing to empirical observation; rather, it depends ... on abstract conceptual relations that he develops in his *Science of Logic*" (p. 818).
[33] In the *Phenomenology of Spirit* Hegel describes the family as a "natural ethical community" and in the *Philosophy of Right* as "immediate or *natural* ethical spirit."
[34] Léon A. Heim in "Natürlicher Sittlicher Geist" argues that the reference to nature unifies the marks of Hegel's concept because the family has as its central task to mediate nature and freedom. While I wouldn't dispute this overall description, I doubt that this makes all marks of the concept of the family necessary.

engage the capacities that we share with nonhuman animals. But this does not tell us all that much about how the family is to be internally structured, nor does it place clear limits on how the concept of the family can change, nor does it exclude the possibility that these problems could be better solved or these capacities better engaged in places other than the family. For this reason, nature will play a subsidiary role in my analysis.

In calling this Element *Hegel on the Family Form,* I want to bring Hegel into conversation with family abolition, but also to signal that my focus will be on the "formal" features that Hegel associates with the family, by which I mean the underlying structures that Hegel takes the family to manifest.[35] In the context of Hegel's account, "family form" can be understood in two ways. On the one hand, family form refers to these underlying structures that are discernible in, though irreducible to, the determinate relationships among family members. On the other hand, family form also refers to these determinate relationships themselves, relationships that have assumed a specific shape in time. I could have called the volume "Hegel on the Idea of the Family," since "idea" in Hegel's technical sense captures both meanings. As Hegel puts it in the Introduction to the *Philosophy of Right,* "Philosophy has to do with ideas and therefore not with what are commonly described as *mere concepts* ... The *shape* [*Gestaltung*] which the concept assumes in its actualization, and which is essential for cognition of the concept itself, is different from its *form* [*Form*] of being purely as concept" (PR §1). So "form" here is meant to be another term for this "shape" which the concept – in this case the concept *of the family* – assumes in its actualization.

The Element is divided into three parts, each organized around one of the three relations that Hegel associates with the family as an existing and evolving institution: that between brothers and sisters, that between husbands and wives, and that between parents and children. What Hegel shows is that we can find out a lot about the family if we take the brother–sister, the husband–wife, and the parent–child relationships as our objects of analysis. Again, my focus will be on the underlying structures that Hegel takes these relationships to manifest, rather than on the relationships per se, which can themselves be said to range from more to less contingent, with the brother–sister relationship representing one end of the spectrum and the parent–child relationship representing the other. In each case, I will ask which aspects Hegel takes to be indispensable and which aspects inessential for the realization of the freedom that the family should provide. And in each case, I will argue that Hegel does not rule out a radical

---

[35] An alternative would have been to frame my discussion in terms of "functions" that the family as an institution is to fulfill. Hegel often appeals to analogies between social orders and living organism, since he conceives of social orders as organized into institutional "organs" with coordinated functions.

transformation of the family along the lines that family abolitionists would like to see. This is a surprising position from the perspective of Hegel scholarship. Just to be clear, I am not denying that Hegel is undoubtedly not calling for the abolition of the family. What I am claiming is only that his account of the family turns out to be more open to family abolition than it might initially seem.

It is worth noting that Hegel introduces these three relationships in his *Phenomenology of Spirit* (PhG ¶456), rather than in his *Philosophy of Right*. Reading these two texts alongside each other can offer a fuller picture of Hegel's family form, for they jointly underscore the extent to which Hegel sees the family as the result of a process during which the concept changed over time.[36] These two texts also include the main passages in which Hegel addresses the "feminine" [*das Weibliche*] and the "masculine" [*das Männliche*] as a difference imbued with social significance. This has made its key passages focal points for feminist interpretations of Hegel's work.[37] Although this is a volume about Hegel's concept of the family, not Hegel on women, the two cannot be fully separated.[38] One of the questions I am pursuing in the following is how to approach Hegel from a feminist point of view if one wants to remain true to his project.[39] I would like to understand the situation of women in Hegel's account of the family and what this situation tells us about Hegel's views about women and about the family.[40] While Hegel officially favored confining women to the home and saddling them with its maintenance, I recommend that we read him closely, even if irreverently, with a willingness take his texts in directions that he himself probably could not have imagined and likely would not have desired.[41]

---

[36] For a more detailed study of the historical development of the family, see Bockenheimer, *Hegels Familien- und Geschlechtertheorie*.

[37] Hegel is talking primarily about the bourgeois nuclear family in early nineteenth-century Prussia, which means that his account of women applies only to white women in this social and historical situation. In his *Lectures on the Philosophy of World History,* does provide an example from the Congo of a female-ruled state.

[38] The three relationships I mentioned above seem to imply a sexual difference between the relata, including the relationship between parent and child, which Hegel first introduces as a relationship between mother and son.

[39] There have been multiple taxonomies for feminist readings of the canon, specifically of Hegel as the paradigmatic canonical figure. The most influential is Seyla Benhabib's distinction between the "good father," the "rebellious daughter," and the "feminist discourse of empowerment" in "On Hegel, Women, and Irony." See also Kimberly Hutchings' taxonomy in *Hegel and Feminist Philosophy*. For other feminist approaches to Hegel, see Hutchings & Pulkkinen (eds.), *Hegel's Philosophy and Feminist Thought,* Patricia J. Mills (ed.), *Feminist Interpretations of G.W.F. Hegel*, and Jean-Baptiste Vuillerod, *Hegel Féministe*.

[40] I have in mind a reading that focuses on aspects of Hegel's texts that are of interest to feminists, whether these are positive or negative for feminist purposes. I don't mean a reading that either criticizes Hegel for falling short of feminist standards or that praises Hegel for being a feminist in disguise.

[41] Some people draw a sharp divide between 'past-centered' vs. "present-centered" (Rorty) or "antiquarian" vs. "anachronistic" (Beiser) approaches to the history of philosophy. I am

I am grateful to Sebastian Stein and Joshua Wretzel for commissioning this Element. Thanks to the participants in the workshop on "Hegel's Antigone" with Gregor Moder organized by New Yugoslav Studies at UC Berkeley, the workshop on "Hegel und die Familie" at HU Berlin, the workshop on "Hegel on Kinship and Reproduction" organized by Ana Maria Miranda Mora and Karen Koch, Rahel Jaeggi's colloquium at the HU Berlin and Andrea Kern's colloquium at the University of Leipzig for helpful discussions. Thanks especially to Livia von Samson for many suggestions about family abolition, and to Katie Coyne and Syan Lopez for many conversations about Hegel and the family. My greatest gratitude goes to Federica Gregoratto, Thimo Heisenberg, Rolf Horstmann, Andrea Kern, Karen Ng, and Francey Russell for feedback on earlier drafts and for their support of this project.

2 Brothers and Sisters

"It was the sad privilege of blood relations to love him despite all."
-Marilynne Robinson, *Home*

Natural Communities

When people resort to the proverbial saying that blood is thicker than water, they are usually expressing what they take to be a valuable feature of family relations, namely, that they are non-optional, i.e. that we do not choose our own families.[42] This fact is supposed to make family relations more enduring than, say, friendships. It is also supposed to show that families enable an appreciation of individuals as non-fungible, non-substitutable. Someone persuaded by this line of thinking might ask: Where else will you find connections to other people who see you as unlike anyone else and who will not stop relating to you irrespective of what you accomplish or fail to accomplish, because they are literally related to you whether they like it or not?

At first sight, Hegel adheres to such a line of thinking. From Hegel's point of view, the fact that family membership is non-optional indicates an important difference between the family and civil society. In civil society, we either compete with others for rewards or we affiliate with them due to common interests. What makes the family different is not just that you cannot easily sever or deny the relationships that you bear to your relatives, but also that you cannot easily opt out of the shared projects to which you as a member

---

following Genevieve Lloyd in rejecting this binary. As Lloyd puts it, "Attention to authorial context and engagement with the present reinforce one another. But it is not surprising that the conjunction should prove an obstacle in the reception of feminist history of philosophy" ("Feminism in History of Philosophy," pp. 258–259).

[42] In light of this intuition, the term "chosen family" can sound like an oxymoron.

contribute. This brings family membership closer to citizenship, which is intended to be similarly lasting. But unlike the state, your family ideally values you in your idiosyncratic entirety, as the distinctive person that you are.[43] Hegel calls this your "singular individuality" [*einzelne Individualität*].

Indeed, when Hegel first introduces the concept of the family into the *Phenomenology of Spirit*, he calls the family a "natural ethical community" [*natürliches sittliches Gemeinwesen*] (PhG ¶449), defining the family in both natural and ethical terms. Hegel is thereby establishing a connection between blood ties (the natural side of the family) on the one hand, and singular individuality (the ethical side of the family) on the other. But the concept of the family changes in the course of Hegel's chapter. The initial concept of the family is one to which a blood tie is essential and singular individuality is at best incidental: to constitute a family is to be related by blood, whether or not you recognize one another as singular individuals. The point can be put even more forcefully, for Hegel even thinks this initial concept of the family is unequipped to accommodate singular individuality. The concept of the family with which we end is one to which singular individuality is essential and a blood tie is incidental: to constitute a family is to recognize one another as singular individuals whether or not you are related by blood. This provides an example of a conceptual change in what counts as a family that will carry over into Hegel's *Philosophy of Right*.

In this first section, I will track how Hegel arrives at the conclusion that singular individuality is a part of the concept of the family and that families are thus institutions to which singular individuality must be central. Here my emphasis will be on singular individuality as a structural feature of the family that Hegel takes to be necessary for the realization of freedom, whether or not it turns out to be the case that this structural feature must be instantiated in family relations and could not be realized in other ways. By singular individuality, I mean something more than the "logical" category of singularity [*Einzelheit*], which Hegel articulated in the *Science of Logic*. Individuals in this "logical" sense are whatever is an individuated manifestation of general kinds. But when Hegel claims that families are spaces for the flourishing of singular individuality, he means that family members are not to be reduced to tokens of types, but are to be appreciated as irreplaceably unique, beings whose loss cannot be compensated. Distinctive of Hegel's defense of the family is his claim that singular individuality in this more demanding sense had first to emerge as a publicly acknowledged principle before it could become recognized within the family and before it could become a part of its concept.

---

[43] For a discussion of the differences between the unity of the family and the unity of the state, see Neuhouser's *Foundations of Hegel's Social Theory*, p. 138.

What makes Hegel's argument so original is that it arrives at singular individuality as a feature of the family form by examining the brother–sister relationship in particular.[44] Hegel himself had a sister with whom he enjoyed an especially close bond. But it seems to be wholly contingent, a matter of sheer good or bad luck, whether people end up having brothers or sisters. When Hegel first introduces the concept of the family into the *Phenomenology of Spirit*, he nevertheless places the relationship between brothers and sisters at its center. According to Hegel, it is the brother–sister relationship that represents the ethical kernel of the family and that generates the highest duties of which this institution is capable, surpassing even those that bind parents and children and husbands and wives. In light of their prominence in the *Phenomenology of Spirit*, it is striking that brothers and sisters are then absent from Hegel's description of the family in the *Philosophy of Right*, in which the family shrinks to the size of the nuclear household, reduced to husband, wife, and child. So, why does Hegel take the brother–sister relation to be initially central to the family and subsequently irrelevant to it?

We can begin to answer this question by noting that this chapter is setting the stage for Hegel's reading of Sophocles' *Antigone*. *Antigone* is an ancient Greek tragedy in which a young woman named Antigone defies the king Creon's edict by burying her brother, Polyneices, despite the fact that Creon had labelled him a traitor and decreed that his corpse be left exposed. What I want to suggest is that Hegel's reading of *Antigone* traces how the concept of the family was shaped by a historical process, specifically how the singular individuality of living family members became an integral part of the family form. There are two reasons that Hegel's reconstruction of this process is relevant for our purposes. First, Hegel is making a case for thinking the blood ties among family members are insufficient for the recognition of singular individuality. Second, Hegel is making the case for thinking that singular individuality cannot be recognized if the family is taken in isolation from other social institutions, which already unsettles any sharp distinction between private and public. What Hegel's reading of *Antigone* reveals is the extent to which the family is embedded in a broader context on which it depends. In the absence of public support for its underlying principle, the family cannot succeed as a distinct sphere in which freedom is realized.

I will argue that it is Antigone in particular who discovers singular individuality *for the first time* so-to-speak in the guise of her brother, Polyneices. This makes singular individuality the fruit of a process that Hegel calls "experience"

---

[44] As Francey Russell has pointed out to me, even psychoanalysis has had surprisingly little to say about siblings. This makes Hegel's focus on siblingship even more remarkable.

[*Erfahrung*]. Hegel interprets the brother–sister relation as a unique place within the family understood as a "natural ethical community" that allows for the full expression of individuality, and so allows individuality in this full sense to break into a world that had made no prior room for it. Once it has been discovered, however, singular individuality can become a structural feature of the family and can come to permeate other relationships as well, in principle even those beyond the family. Such an approach will allow us to capture the repercussions of Antigone's deed: although Antigone is single-mindedly focused on just this one brother, she discovers something with universal implications, even if these implications exceed her immediate concerns: that all individuals are singular and deserve to be recognized as such.[45] Through his reading of this literary text, Hegel is emphasizing that our modern understanding of how families are constituted and what makes them valuable has its source in historical experience.[46]

Singular Individuality

When Hegel first introduces brothers and sisters, he distinguishes them from husbands and wives as well as parents and children. Here is the key passage that needs to be explained: "In the ethical household, it is not a question of *this* particular husband, *this* particular child, but simply of husband and children generally; the relationships of the woman are based, not on feeling, but on the universal ... The loss of the brother is therefore irreparable to the sister and her duty towards him is the highest" (PhG ¶457). In the ethical household it is not a question of *this* particular husband or *this* particular child, but of *a* husband or *a* child. When it comes to a brother, "this particular brother" by contrast counts, which is why the loss of a brother is to a sister "irreparable." Although Hegel does not name her, there is little doubt that the passage is a reference to the way in which Antigone interpreted her familial relations and the way in which she ranked her role obligations. Hegel is articulating a rule on the basis of which Antigone understood herself to be duty bound to bury her brother, even if this rule would not make her duty bound to bury her husband or child.[47]

---

[45] Alenka Zupancic in *Let Them Rot* has argued against a universalistic reading of Antigone, since Antigone is not claiming that all human beings should be treated like singular individuals, only that her one brother should. What I am saying is that the singular individuality of all human beings is an implication of her claim.

[46] According to Terry Pinkard in *Sociality of Reason*, Hegel's chapter is criticizing a modern fantasy about the Greeks, rather than the historical Greeks. It is also worth pointing out that Hegel is not making a narrowly historical claim about how singular individuality was as a matter of fact discovered in real time. Antigone is after all a literary character and her world does not correspond exactly or accurately to the world of the ancient Greeks.

[47] Burial suggests one important way in which the family is designed to provide a solution to a problem that stems from our nature as living creatures: *what to do with the dead*. But Hegel also

Hegel's formulation is an allusion to a passage in Sophocles' play, uttered by Antigone: "Suppose I had been a mother and a widow. I would not have taken this burden on or defied the nation, in that case. The principle I followed is this: if my husband had died, there might be another, and a son by another man if I had lost my children. But my mother and father were gone. I could never have had a new brother."[48] Antigone is making a similar point to the one that Hegel ascribes to her, which is that the loss of a husband or a child would not affect her as deeply as the loss of a brother. But her explanation is difficult to understand.[49] What she is saying is that she can always marry a different man, and have another child, but that *because her parents are already dead,* she can never have a new brother. It makes her rule contingent on the fact that her parents happen to be dead and that she herself happens to be of a child-bearing age. If her parents were not already dead, would this bear on her duty to bury her brother? If she could not bear another child, would this raise her child's importance in her eyes? Be that as it may, I want to focus on Hegel's reason for including a version of this passage, which indicates what Hegel takes to be the relevant difference between the brother–sister relation on the one hand, and other familial relations on the other.

Hegel's passage has drawn scholarly attention for its gendered perspective, for Hegel is not implying that any of Antigone's brothers (and she had in fact three: Polyneices, Eteocles, and Oedipus who is also her father) would have been inclined to make a similar assertion.[50] The brother–sister relation is asymmetrical, generating duties for sisters that brothers do not reciprocate. One reason for this gendered perspective has to do with the fact that women are confined to the ethical household as the guardians of the "divine law."[51] But another reason has to do with the requirement of recognition [*Anerkennung*], which Hegel develops in the course of the *Phenomenology*. Hegel is here asking

---

makes clear that burial is anything but a natural process – in fact, its aim to wrest the family member away from natural decay.

[48] Sophocles, p. 56, 1060–1065.

[49] According to Zupancic's reading, Antigone is saying that everyone is replaceable, but not all people are reproducible, and that this un-reproducibility has to do with the fact that her father is also her brother, Oedipus. I put the question of incest aside since it does not figure in Hegel's interpretation of the tragedy.

[50] Jean B. Elshtain writes (in *Public Man, Private Woman*) that Hegel should have known that no one "can have a relationship with an abstract category" (p. 177). But as Susanne Brauer has already pointed out in *Natur* und *Sittlichkeit,* Hegel isn't saying that anyone has a relationship with a "husband-in-general" or "children-in-general." Although Antigone would have married only one husband, Hegel's point is that she would see this husband as only the token of a type, not a singular individual in the relevant sense.

[51] There is a lot of debate around what Hegel means by the divine law, whether it even counts as a law (Butler), and whether it is the law of the family or rather a Greek law that transcends the boundaries of the city-state (Harris). This set of questions is orthogonal to my topic in this section.

how Antigone can receive the recognition that she requires in the context of her household in order to become a self-conscious subject, a question that would not arise for her brother, who can receive recognition elsewhere. Without recognition, Antigone would be unable to conceive of herself as an ethical agent, someone who is bound by the divine law.[52] And without recognition, Antigone would not be a free agent in the sense that she would not have an opportunity to exercise freedom, which requires seeing others as integral to freedom's realization.

This notion of recognition assumes a prominent role at this juncture in the *Phenomenology* and becomes pivotal to Hegel's conception of the family as a sphere of freedom. Hegel in fact appeals to recognition when he seeks to explain the importance of the brother–sister relation. Just before he describes the loss of the brother as "irreparable," Hegel writes,

> The brother, however, if for the sister a passive, similar being in general; the recognition of herself in him is pure and unmixed with any natural desire. In this relationship, therefore, the indifference of the particularity, and the ethical contingency of the latter, are not present; but the moment of the individual self, recognizing and being recognized, can here assert its right, because it is linked to the equilibrium of blood and is a relation devoid of desire. (PhG ¶457)

It suggests that there is something about brothers that makes the recognition that a woman can receive from them qualitatively different from other forms of recognition possible within the family. Such a statement confirms the common impression that Hegel considers the brother–sister relation to be the best kind of relationship to a man that a woman can hope to achieve.[53] But what is it about brothers that makes the relationship that women bear to them uniquely satisfying, or at least more satisfying than the other available options?

Hegel provides two possible answers. First, a brother is a "similar being in general," standing on a relatively equal footing to a sister, a point of difference from parental and spousal relations, since both of those involve a higher degree of inequality among the parties. It is not to assume that brothers and sisters are exactly equal, for one major asymmetry between them is that sisters depend on their brother's recognition and not vice versa. Brothers after all become citizens and are in a position to achieve a publicly valued form of recognition through

---

[52] I make this point in *Hegel on Second Nature in Ethical Life*.
[53] See Patricia J. Mills, "Hegel's *Antigone*," p. 61. George Steiner writes, "Femininity itself, urges Hegel, has its highest intimation, its moral quintessence, in the condition of sorority" (*Antigones*, p. 33). Silvia Locatelli, in "Hegel's Antigone: A Revolutionary Role," argues that the brother–sister relationship provides a model for thinking about sexual difference, because it preserves difference without rooting it in reproduction, which is responsible for a sexual hierarchy.

their role in the state. Second, Hegel stresses that the relationship to a brother is "unmixed by natural desire," namely, that siblings enjoy the benefits of not desiring each other.[54] An absence of natural desire is significant because it allows siblingship to attain a state of "equilibrium."[55] The more obvious contrast would be the spousal relation, which is sexual in nature. But Hegel thinks parenthood is also unstable because it stands on unfirm emotional ground. In a striking passage (PhG ¶456), Hegel describes parents as affected by the fact that children have an independent existence that they as their parents cannot take back, and children as affected by the fact that they live at their parents' expense, becoming living evidence of their parents' mortality.[56]

Simone de Beauvoir suggests a third possible answer. In her feminist classic, *The Second Sex,* Beauvoir refers to Hegel's key passage, arguing that the difference lies in the fact that a woman's femininity is at stake in marriage and motherhood in a way in which it is not at stake in her relationship with her brother. Beauvoir writes, "This points out that for a woman it is not at all a question of establishing individual relations with a chosen husband, but rather of justifying the exercise of her feminine function in their generality."[57] The idea would be that a woman without a husband or without a child is compromised as a woman – her femininity is in question. If this is true, then there is something inevitably generic inscribed into both the spousal and parental relation. These are properly speaking generalizable social roles. What Beauvoir implies is that a woman without a brother would not be compromised in the same way, for she is no less of a woman if she happens to have no brother. The fact that her femininity is not threatened allows her to adopt a special relationship to the brother she happens to have, and to see him as more than an example of a broader social category that she is under pressure to fill.[58]

If we return to the second passage I discussed earlier, we will notice that Hegel explicitly associates kinship grounded in blood with mutual recognition. As he puts it, "recognition and being recognized can here assert its right,

---

[54] Judith Butler in *Antigone's Claim* notes that in the case of recognition between the lord and bondsman desire does play an important role (p. 14).

[55] Luce Irigaray calls this equilibrium the *Hegelian dream*, "a truce in the struggle between uneven foes" in *Speculum of the Other Woman*, p. 217.

[56] This sheds new light on Antigone's statement in the play. She can never have another brother not only because her parents happen to be dead, but also because her parents were destined to die, so that this natural fact about them is integral to the relationship she bears to them.

[57] Beauvoir, *The Second Sex,* p. 450.

[58] In a different context, Hegel is making a similar point: "What does the man want, the girl? She a husband, he a wife. She loves him, why? Because he should become her husband, make her a wife; – from him she should receive her honor, her value, her joy, her happiness, as *spouse*" (R §162R). In short, Hegel is saying that a woman is realized as a woman (enjoying honor, value, joy, happiness) when she becomes a husband's wife.

because it is linked to the equilibrium of blood and is a relation devoid of desire" (my emphasis). Hegel is contrasting two different facets of "nature" broadly construed: equilibrium of blood and relation of desire.[59] He is claiming that recognition can "assert its right" because brothers and sisters, even though they are not naturally bound by desire, are naturally bound by blood. One way to understand the significance of blood would be to say that it signals the distinction between inside and outside the family. This would render the brother–sister relation the core of the family as a unit, since brothers and sisters are of the *same* blood, born of the same parents. But blood is also an unhelpful criterion by which to circumscribe families, and as far as symbols go, it is rather diffuse, a liquid that mixes and spreads.[60] A different way to understand the significance of blood would be to say that blood is supposed to represent the non-optional character of siblingship, for brothers and sisters are thrown into a single family whether they like it or not. The fact that they are kin in a natural sense is presumably relevant to establishing the needed equilibrium between them because it fortifies their relationship, making it enduring. It is not up to either of them whether the other comes to be, making a brother a kind of abundance, a gift from nature that cannot be compelled or guaranteed.[61]

Although Hegel is drawing a connection between kinship and recognition, he is not implying that the former is either necessary to or sufficient for the latter. The term Hegel uses is *verknüpft* – linked, associated. A blood tie plays a role in the process in which mutual recognition comes to assert its right, but once mutual recognition has asserted its right, it is no longer so obvious that it continues to rely on a blood tie. A blood tie is moreover insufficient for mutual recognition. Consider the fact that Sophocles' play features a different sister, Ismene, for whom a brother is not comparably irreplaceable. Ismene is another woman of the same family, so also a relative of both Antigone and Polyneices, but does not consider herself to be to duty bound to bury her brother under these circumstances. Many have remarked on the fact that Hegel does not refer to Ismene in his reading of the play, and some have suggested that he should have considered the sister–sister relation.[62] I take Hegel to be making an indirect allusion to Ismene by emphasizing the fact that Antigone is not merely fulfilling her sisterly duty, thereby calling to mind the contrasting example of Ismene

---

[59] Cynthia Willett, in "Hegel, Antigone, and the Possibility of Ecstatic Dialogue," argues that Hegel cannot purge desire from the brother–sister relation, because it is only desire that can explain why Antigone prioritizes her brother in a singular way. I see no evidence of this in Hegel's text.

[60] In "The Eternal Irony of the Community," Irigaray draws out the associations with blood, emphasizing that blood is a liquid that cannot be contained or managed, which makes it an apt metaphor for sexual difference.

[61] Thanks to Andrea Kern for this formulation.   [62] Mills, "Hegel's *Antigone*," p. 76.

without explicitly mentioning her. Hegel's reading makes clear that being of the same blood does not yet ensure that you will see your brother as not just a brother, but as *this* brother. In order to come to see her brother in this way, Antigone had to exceed the demands of her social role, which she does by making an unparalleled discovery.[63]

Antigone's Experience

I now turn to my central thesis in this section, which is that Antigone came to see her brother as this brother because she discovers something that does not fit into her social world – "the principle of singular individuality as such" (¶473). The background to my reading of this chapter is Hegel's method outlined in the Introduction, according to which conceptual changes arise through a process that Hegel calls *experience*. Experience for Hegel has a negative and a positive dimension. Negatively speaking, experiences are lived episodes that involve despair, frustration, even suffering, because they challenge a given framework, overturning assumptions about the constitution of the world. Positively speaking, experiences are lived episodes that provoke innovation because they disclose new objects, or new features of an object, thereby confronting us with previously unavailable aspects of reality and compelling us to expand our concepts or develop new concepts in order to capture what we discover. This process of experience becomes more complex in the context of the Spirit-chapter, in which Hegel's reading of *Antigone* is situated. In this Spirit-chapter, we are no longer dealing with a single "consciousness" that confronts an object other than itself, but with conflicting perspectives among subjects about a shared world they jointly inhabit. As I read the Spirit-chapter, it presents us with a learning process in which some have experiences of which others remain deprived, despite the fact that all of them belong to one "shape of spirit" and so avail themselves of a common conceptual framework. We find that it is Antigone in particular who is undergoing this process of experience in Hegel's double-sided sense.

The negative dimension of experience is on stark display in Sophocles' play. After Creon issues the verdict that Antigone is to be buried alive, everything around him falls apart. The play presents the tragic collapse of a world by showing the disintegration of a politically significant household. This negative dimension of experience is also on stark display in Hegel's reading of the play. According to his reading, both Antigone and Creon committed a crime, because

---

[63] This is a feature of ancient ethical life, in which acting ethically required going beyond generic social requirements. Hegel emphasizes that in modern ethical life, exceptional virtue is replaced by rectitude.

each of them violated a law that was equally essential to their shared world. By refusing to return Polyneices' corpse to his relatives, Creon violated the divine law, which demands that the family perform burial rites for kin.[64] By burying her brother, Antigone in turn violated the human law, which is under Creon's jurisdiction. It is crucial to Hegel's interpretation that Antigone and Creon are both in the wrong.[65] In this respect he departs from the play itself, which places the blame squarely on Creon's shoulders. The reason that this equality in guilt is crucial to Hegel's interpretation is that he takes this specific set of failures – the crimes committed, the sufferings incurred – to incriminate the social order as a whole, and hence the framework that Antigone and Creon shared. If their conflict could in principle be adjudicated within this framework, it would leave the framework itself intact.

Hegel distills this negative moment of experience in a line he plucks from the play: "Because we suffer, we recognize that we have erred" [*Weil wir leiden, anerkennen wir, dass wir gefehlt*] (PhG ¶469). It is a line uttered by Antigone, in which she is describing suffering as informative, illuminating, an opportunity for learning that a mistake has been made. In Hegel's rendition of the line, the mistake could not have been avoided, and so the suffering could not have been averted, because the worldview in question was fundamentally inadequate. The German word is "*gefehlt*," which suggests not only missing the mark, but also missing something, indicating a lack or an absence. Hegel offers the following diagnosis: "This demise of ethical substance and its transition into another shape is determined, as a result, by this: That ethical consciousness is *immediately* directed towards the law, and this determination of immediacy means that nature itself enters into ethical life's action" (PhG ¶475). Here he is expressing two interrelated reasons for thinking that the framework was fundamentally inadequate and hence doomed to disintegrate: the immediate relationship of ethical consciousness to the law, which in turn granted nature a role in ethical action. In short, its fatal flaw was its reliance on natural considerations in the assignment of social obligations in order to ensure the immediacy of allegiance.[66] It is clear that Hegel is offering this diagnosis with the benefit of hindsight, going beyond what Antigone and Creon could have learned from their own suffering. What Antigone's line expresses is an admission that something has gone awry, not yet a full grasp of the source of error.

---

[64] It ends up being the gods who "rise up in hostility and destroy the community which has dishonored and shattered its own power, the sacred claims of the family" (PhG 474).

[65] I am disagreeing with Mills' interpretation, according to which Hegel makes Creon into the "hero of the play" (p. 70) and the "just representative of the law of the polis" (p. 75). I am also disagreeing with Willett, who claims that to "interpret their crimes as equal is already to favor Creon, or at least his appeal to the rights of community" (p. 279).

[66] PhG 476.

The line in question is framed as a collective lesson, put in terms of a "we," which is in keeping with Hegel's emphasis on the fact that both Antigone and Creon are agents of a crime and patients of suffering, on equal footing on that front. But it is Antigone, not Creon, who is a position to state this collective lesson. Antigone has an epistemic advantage because she is discovering an aspect of the world that had not yet become incorporated, something that points beyond the limits of their shared framework. Before Antigone comes on the scene, Greek ethical life as Hegel describes it did already include families as natural ethical communities, so it already contained families as kinship relations that involve duties toward family members. But before Antigone comes to the scene, Greek ethical life did not provide resources for grasping singular individuality as a genuine feature of reality, a feature that needs to be acknowledged and accommodated. It is telling that in Hegel's description of the ancient family, a member could become recognized as singular individual only once deceased:

> Therefore the action, which embraces the entire existence of blood relations, has as its object and content the singular individual – not the citizen, for he does not belong to the family, nor does it have the singular individual who is to become a citizen and is supposed to *cease* counting as *this singular individual* – but rather, it has as the object the individual who as *this* singular individual belongs to the family, and who as a universal being, is exempted from his sensuous, i.e. singular activity. The action no longer concerns the *living* but rather the *dead*. (PhG ¶450)

It means that singular individuality had been banished to the netherworld, allowed to exist only as a "non-actual shadow" [*unwirkliche Schatten*] (PhG ¶467).[67]

Although Antigone discovers singular individuality in her brother only after he is no longer among the living, Hegel also claims that she has a hunch [*Ahnung*] of what is ethical in a way that exceeds Creon's grasp.[68] It is tempting to think that Hegel is relying on sexist stereotypes, claiming that women are by nature intuitive.[69] As I read him, Hegel is instead making a claim about the

---

[67] The fact that the object of the family is not the living, but the dead is supposed to explain how it came to be that the act of burial assumes such importance. By burying the dead, you are recognizing family members as more than tokens of types in a way in which you could not recognize them as such while they were still alive.

[68] "The family, in the form of the sister, has the highest intuitive awareness [*höchste Ahnung*] of what is ethical. She does not attain to *consciousness* of it, or to the objective existence of it" (PhG 457).

[69] Willett describes this as a "shadowy kind of knowledge" that "can only be partially brought to consciousness or submitted to a rational dialectic" (p. 282). But Antigone's knowledge is "shadowy" only under specific circumstances, and it even becomes the driving force of the "rational dialectic." I also worry that this way of characterizing Antigone's knowledge comes dangerously close to the view that there are essentially "feminine" ways of knowing.

status of the object that the sister apprehends when she recognizes her brother as a singular individual. If the singular individual is at most an "unreal shadow," then it is in principle impossible to have a conscious relation to him, for singular individuality is not yet a real object, and hence a possible object for consciousness. This means that Antigone does not have singular individuality before her in the shape of a living individual in such a way that it could be an object for her. But what she discovers through her deceased brother allows her to demand that the singular individuality of those who are living be publicly acknowledged. If Antigone's relationship to singular individuality is not yet "conscious," this is due to the nature of her object, not due to the kind of cognition of which she as a woman is capable. Rather than falling short of the standards of consciousness, Antigone has a premonition of something that is only now emerging out of the darkness of the "netherworld." And a premonition is all that anyone can have of that which has not yet become publicly acknowledged as genuinely real.

Hegel infamously calls womankind the "eternal irony" and "internal enemy" of the community. Hegel adds,

> In this way, the feminine turns to ridicule the solemn wisdom of maturity, which, being dead to singular individuality ... only thinks of and is concerned for the universal. The feminine turns this mature wisdom into an object of ridicule for immature, high-minded youths and into the object of contempt for those youths' enthusiasm. As such, she elevates the force of youth into the status of what is validly established. (PhG ¶474)

Although Hegel is here speaking about women in general, we can understand this as an effort to elaborate the implications of Antigone's discovery. If "womankind" turns out to be the "eternal irony" and "internal enemy" of the community, this is due to the fact that Antigone has defended the principle of singular individuality and demanded that it be accommodated in a living way, even though this cannot be achieved within the constraints of her community, which is "dead" to the principle and designed to "suppress" it. In this passage, Hegel is once again alluding to the brother–sister relation as that place within the family where Antigone was able to make her case. Because she is excluded from public life, however, she can only make this case by treating that which the state does value with contempt. Her effort to meet her duty to just this one brother becomes an action with sweeping reverberations. But it is her community that has turned her into an irony and an enemy, putting her in a position in which she had no other option.[70]

---

[70] Hegel is not implying that this is going to be true of any community, so that women are in principle condemned to political exclusion. According to my reading, she is an internal enemy as long as the principle of singular individuality has been suppressed. In calling her irony "eternal," Hegel is perhaps suggesting that there is a persistent tension between singular individuality and what can be publicly recognized by an institution like the state.

Hegel's Antigone has captured the imagination of a long line of scholars, particularly those who have searched for ways to read Hegel from a feminist point of view. As Carol Jacobs has put it: "No red-blooded woman, after all, can fail to enjoy the irony of wearing Hegel's slur as something of a crown."[71] It has remained an ongoing debate whether Hegel conceives of Antigone as a complex ethical agent who takes charge of her own fate or dismisses her as an unreflective adherent of the divine law. Feminist readings of Hegel's chapter have wavered between criticizing Hegel for his limited understanding of Antigone or lauding Hegel for giving us a portrait of a figure who rebels not only against Creon, but maybe even against Hegel himself. Should we read Antigone with Hegel, against Hegel, or (as Karin de Boer has recommended) "with and against Hegel"?[72] Here are two influential readings that model the last option. Luce Irigaray has read this chapter as arguing that the "masculine" state must exclude and repress the "feminine" domain of the family, without which it cannot function but which it cannot incorporate.[73] And Judith Butler has read this chapter as showing that Antigone threatens such distinctions, for she reveals that kinship is always contaminated by politics, which impacts whose loss can be legitimately grieved.[74]

Inspired by a tradition in feminist philosophy known as standpoint theory, I am recommending interpreting Antigone as a knower at the vanguard of her shape of spirit.[75] What makes Hegel's Antigone a "feminist" figure, to the extent to which it makes sense to describe her in these terms, is her pioneering insight into a previously unavailable aspect of her world. She is ahead of her time, catching a glimpse of something that is only in the process of taking shape.[76] When Hegel claims that Antigone acts knowingly, he means not only that she knows she is violating the human law and so knows what awaits her. Rather, her action is guided by an insight into the structure of her world, for her experience gives her access to a new kind of object, a singular individual, for which her framework has not equipped her or her contemporaries. It is in order to articulate what she has discovered that she is compelled to transgress the boundaries to which she has been officially confined, stepping out of the family and pursuing a political course of action. Despite the fact that Hegel wants to emphasize the extent to which both

---

[71] Jacobs, "Dusting Antigone," pp. 889–890. [72] De Boer, "Hegel's Antigone," p. 141.

[73] See Irigaray, "The Eternal Irony of the Community." See also Elena Tzelepis, "Antigone's Dissidence," referring to Antigone as representing the "essential outside" (p. 261).

[74] According to Butler in *Antigone's Claim*, it is a political question "which social arrangements can be recognized as legitimate love, and which human losses can be explicitly grieved as real and consequential losses" (p. 24).

[75] For example, Mills thinks that Hegel's dialectical process excludes Antigone because Hegel prioritizes the universal over the particular. I am instead suggesting that Antigone in fact moves Hegel's dialectical process forward, playing a role analogous to that of the 'bondsman' in the dialectic of lordship and bondage.

[76] I am primarily thinking of Sandra Harding, Nancy Hartsock, and Joan Scott.

Creon and Antigone acted one-sidedly, Hegel ultimately gives greater weight to Antigone's perspective, since it is Antigone that is undergoing an experience of which others remain deprived. This puts Antigone and Creon on unequal footing as far as learning is concerned, with one of them discovering aspects of the world that the other is not yet in a position to grasp.

My reading also allows us to explain why Hegel grants the brother–sister relation center stage. Hegel focuses on the brother–sister relation not because he thinks that all families should include it, or because he thinks that a family is incomplete without it, but because he wants to show that there are indeed reasons why Antigone discovered singular individuality as an integral feature of the family by means of her brother, and not by some other means. Given the special nature of the brother–sister relationship, it turned out to be uniquely conducive to her discovery. What puts Antigone in this privileged position to discover this unanticipated feature of reality is not the fact that she is a woman in general, or that she is the female member of a family, though her gender is indeed relevant. Her great advantage is she is a sister, *this* sister in relation to *this* brother, a brother that she comes to see as unlike any other. It is this completely contingent fact about her that allows her to make a discovery of a wholly new structure.

In this way Hegel's Antigone harnesses her kinship relations and her position within the family in order to change the concept of the family from that of a natural ethical community essentially bound by blood ties to that of a natural ethical community to which a recognition of singular individuality is essential. But Hegel's Antigone also challenges the family as a self-enclosed sphere, for she exposes that a broader social context is needed in order to give singular individuality its proper due. Her discovery can lead in two different directions. It can support the idea that the state should be involved in maintaining the family as a distinct social sphere, an idea that Hegel explicitly pursues in the *Philosophy of Right*. Or it can support a different idea, namely, that the family cannot maintain itself as a distinct social sphere without "bleeding" into other spheres, thereby eroding its boundaries. Antigone herself represents at best an ambivalent advocate for the family, for she deliberately refuses to replicate it as she found it. The family may have been her place of origin, but it was decidedly not her final destination.[77]

3 Husbands and Wives

> "My utopia is equal love, equal love between people of equal value, although value is an approximation for the word I want. Why is it so difficult?"
>
> -Norman Rush, *Mating*

---

[77] I am inspired by Butler's formulation that Antigone chooses "the tomb as her wedding chamber," p. 76.

Love as Freedom

Marriage in particular has garnered more critics than the family in general.[78] Even if you believe that the family should be preserved in some form or other, you might still be critical of marriage, and you might even favor its abolition. For one, marriage as an institution is founded upon inequality, which continues to haunt its current iterations. For another, marriage as an institution is highly restrictive, seemingly antithetical to free love. Hegel was acutely aware that marriage had its critics, even in his day. For example, he mentions Friedrich Schlegel, whose controversial novel *Lucinde* depicted an affair between an unmarried woman and her married lover in favorable terms. According to Hegel, writers like Schlegel "represent the physical surrender as necessary in order to prove the freedom and intensity of love" (PR ¶164A). In other words, they believed that it is the sexual act, not the wedding ceremony, that is the pinnacle of free love. Hegel even allowed himself the snide remark that this is an "argument with which seducers are not unfamiliar" (PR ¶164A).[79] If free love means love outside of marriage, specifically sex outside of marriage, Hegel did not approve of it, though he was also not immune to its appeal.[80] In his *Philosophy of Right*, Hegel leaves little doubt that he is defending marriage as an institution, going so far as to claim that people have an ethical duty to get married (PR ¶162 R). Although marriage is for the most part "philosophically undertheorized" (to borrow Elizabeth Brake's words), this is not something of which Hegel can be accused.[81]

But Hegel can be described as a proponent of "free love" in a different sense, for he returned repeatedly to the formal affinity between love and freedom throughout his writings. As we have seen, freedom for Hegel consists in being by oneself in another. Hegel was intrigued by the prospect that love could be a privileged way of living freely. He does not want to identify love and freedom too closely, since love presupposes a feeling and hence a partiality that many other free relationships do not. But he suggests that love properly understood is a concrete expression of freedom, and even more strongly, that freedom would be incomplete if it did not include love, its most readily available expression.[82]

---

[78] See Elizabeth Brake and Clare Chambers. They are concerned with the legal status of marriage, which they claim is incompatible with the neutrality of the liberal state.

[79] For Hegel's assessment of *Lucinde*, see David Farrell Krell, "Lucinde's Shame: Hegel, Sensuous Woman, and the Law"; Frances Olsen, "Hegel, Sexual Ethics and the Oppression of Women"; Jay Geller, "Hegel's Self-Conscious Woman," which argues that Hegel's passage about the "eternal irony of the community" prefigures Lucinde.

[80] While in Jena, Hegel had an illegitimate son with his landlady. Here I am not distinguishing between extramarital and premarital sex, though maybe his judgment would have been different in the two cases. Thanks to Léon Heim for pointing this out.

[81] Brake, *Minimizing Marriage*, p. 1.

[82] When Hegel introduces the concept of the free will in the *Philosophy of Right*, he writes, "we already possess this freedom in the form of feeling [*Empfindung*], for example in friendship and

This conception of love as a privileged form of freedom includes love that is non-romantic or non-erotic, but it extends also to the love that Hegel associates with marriage, what Hegel calls *ethical love* [*sittliche Liebe*]. Hegel thinks of ethical love less in terms of intense feelings, which puts him at odds with certain figures that identified such love with passion or attraction. According to Hegel, ethical love is an intimate interpersonal relationship that bears at best a tangential connection to what goes by the name of falling in love. Passion and attraction can motivate a person to embark on an intimate interpersonal relationship, though Hegel raises doubts about whether they provide great reasons to enter into, say, marriage.[83] Irrespective of how an intimate interpersonal relationship originates, ethical love is for Hegel an achievement that, though not indissoluble, is relatively invulnerable to the vicissitudes of passion and attraction.[84]

In this second section, I want to examine what Hegel means by ethical love and why Hegel holds that ethical love is best served by marriage as an institution. My aim is to isolate ethical love from its institutional expression, although I admit that it is not so easy to pry them fully apart.[85] On the one hand, ethical love gives rise to a new entity, the couple, that exceeds the individual members and assumes a life of its own. On the other hand, ethical love must also provide a context for the flourishing of each member's singular individuality. It is for this reason that Hegel describes ethical love as a union that seems at first sight to be "a self-limitation" of two people in relation to each other, but that is in fact "their liberation" (PR ¶162). Ethical love is usually discussed in terms of mutual recognition.[86] What I will emphasize is that ethical love for Hegel consists in an

---

love" (PR §7A). So, friendship and love have a special status because they make this more abstract concept of the free will concretely available to us.

[83] Hegel suggests that arranged marriages may be on the whole more ethical, since they are guided by parental foresight rather than by fleeting feelings. According to Zizek in "Hegel on Marriage," Hegel's reason for considering arranged marriage more ethical is the fact that "in this case, the contingency of the partner is directly and openly assumed." Brake also mentions Hegel's preference for arranged marriage (*Minimizing Marriage,* p. 10). Hegel alludes to arranged marriages in §162 and §162A, but his assessment is ambivalent, because he worries that forcing women to get married against their will shows a low regard for them.

[84] "Since marriage contains the moment of feeling, it is not absolute but unstable [*schwankend*], and contains the possibility of dissolution in itself" (PR §163A).

[85] As Elizabeth Brake writes, "Since Hegel's account attaches moral value to the relationship, it provides a model for such an account (although Hegel's own account restricts marriage to formalized heterosexual relationships)" (Brake, "Love's Paradox: Making Sense of Hegel on Marriage," 83).

[86] Hegel does not even use the term *Anerkennung* in the relevant passage (which Livia von Samson has pointed out to me), but he does speak in terms of "consciousness" and "self-consciousness," terms for knowledge and self-knowledge. Although Gal Katz emphasizes mutual recognition, he also notes that "love is (also) cognitive and, as such, involves knowing one's lover as having a certain status" (Katz, "Love is only between living beings equal in power," 95).

ongoing activity of cognition that is complex and demanding, for it requires knowing oneself and one's partner, but also this new entity, i.e. the life of the couple. It is this ongoing activity of cognition that makes ethical love both valuable and difficult. Hegel's defense of marriage in turn hinges on his ability to show that marriage is conducive to realizing ethical love. Hegel argues that marriage makes ethical love less difficult, because it provides the public context in which ethical love can grow stable. But I want to suggest that Hegel also strews hints for suspecting that marriage makes ethical love more difficult, because it introduces dangers that threaten the activity of cognition central to it.

By marriage, Hegel means minimally a relationship that is exclusive, enduring, and established through a publicly witnessed and mutually binding wedding ceremony, as well as more robustly a relationship that is heterosexual and patriarchal. Although we can distinguish between these minimal and robust aspects of marriage, it is striking that Hegel tries to justify virtually every feature of marriage as an existing institution by appealing to the requirements of ethical love. For example, Hegel claims that the incest taboo furthers ethical love because it demands that those who are to be united by marriage are not already united by blood.[87] It is also worth noting that ethical love becomes the key difference between the modern nuclear family and the ancient extended family. This is Hegel how describes the modern family in particular: "When a marriage takes place, a new family is constituted, and this is self-sufficient for itself in relation to the kinship groups or houses from which it originated; its links with the latter are based on the natural blood relationship, but the new family is based on ethical love" (PR §172). A modern family based on ethical love is founded through marriage, in which the boundary between private and public is more sharply drawn. The relationship between husbands and wives even usurps the place of that between brothers and sisters as the heart of the modern ethical household.[88]

All in all, ethical love and its expression as marriage become central to Hegel's concept of the family in the modern world. So, one question to consider concerns Hegel's identification between ethical love and marriage and his assumption that ethical love is best served by marriage as an institution. But there is also another question to keep in mind, which I will not be able to discuss

---

[87] "Marriage between blood relations is therefore at variance with the concept of marriage as an ethical act of freedom rather than an association based on immediate natural existence [*Natürlichkeit*] and its drives, and hence it is also at variance with genuine natural feeling [*Empfindung*]" (PR 168).

[88] Marriage is supposed to render the bond between husband and wife similarly or nearly non-optional, comparable to that between siblings. But Hegel does not rule out divorce, though he claims that "legislations must make such dissolution as difficult as possible and uphold the right of the ethical against caprice" (PR §163A).

in this context: Why does Hegel privilege ethical love over other forms of love (such as friendship) and what consequences does this have for the flexibility of his concept of a family? Whether or not ethical love culminates in a lifelong marriage, it is clear that ethical love culminates in a long-term couple. I hope to show that Hegel provides us with some reasons for thinking that ethical love so understood is uniquely valuable from the perspective of freedom. But Hegel clearly does not question the assumption, which has come under scrutiny today, that our lives should be organized around the long-term couple.[89] When compared to the other two goods (singular individuality and material resources), there might be something about ethical love as Hegel understands it that presents a more serious obstacle to a radical transformation of the family. But maybe this calls for scaling back its centrality, rather than abandoning it all together.

Ethical Love

Hegel's interest in the affinity between love and freedom can be traced back to his early fragment on love, in which Hegel sketches a conception of love as a union that both overcomes and preserves a separation between lovers. Hegel claims that "genuine love excludes all opposition"; in case any initial separation does remain, it will be met with shame, which Hegel describes as a "raging of love against [exclusive] individuality." But Hegel also claims that in love "the separate does still remain, but as something united and no longer as something separate."[90] This early fragment places considerable emphasis on the formal structure of love as a distinct kind of relation, which is isomorphic to the relation of freedom. Both are what Hegel will go on to call being by oneself in (or at home with) another. But the fragment is striking for two reasons. One is Hegel's insistence that love cannot be understood merely as a union – it must be a union that maintains an internal difference.[91] Another is Hegel's addition of two substantive constraints on what he is willing to call love. He writes that "true union, or love proper, exists only between living things who are alike in power and thus in one another's eyes living from every point of view."[92] Here Hegel claims that love in the true sense of that term is only possible between two

---

[89] Here I am thinking of Elizabeth Brake's concept of "amatonormativity." Even if Hegel's position is not inherently "heteronormative," the worry might be that it is inherently "amatonormative." I am grateful to both Thimo Heisenberg and Livia von Samson for pressing me on this issue.
[90] Hegel, "Love Fragment."
[91] In *Love Troubles*, Federica Gregoratto distinguishes between union theories and recognition theories of love, but she also acknowledges that Hegel's view includes elements of both.
[92] "Wahre Vereinigung, eigentliche Liebe findet nur unter Lebendigen statt, die an Macht sich gleich, und also durchaus füreinander lebendige, von keiner Seite gegeneinander tote sind."

equally powerful beings and two beings who are to one another thoroughly alive, not in the least bit dead.

This formal structure from the early fragment is then repurposed in his *Science of Logic,* in which Hegel even employs the phrase "free love": "The universal is therefore free power; it is itself while reaching out to its other and embracing it, but without doing violence to it; on the contrary, it is at rest in its other as in its own. Just as it has been called free power, it could also be called free love and boundless blessedness, for it relates to that which is distinct from it as to itself; in it, it has returned to itself."[93] Here Hegel is drawing an analogy between the universal concept and free love, an analogy that exploits this isomorphism between love and freedom. What makes the universal concept comparable to free love is that it exhibits an overcoming of all oppositions. Hegel moreover call this universal concept a "free power" because it embraces its other without violating it, so without imposing itself upon something that resists it. Although he does not mention equality in this passage, we can think of this nonviolent form of power as a relationship that is reciprocal and symmetrical, a relationship among comparable elements. Here Hegel also foregrounds this structure of union, all the while emphasizing that a difference between the two elements must be maintained. For a loving relationship to obtain, that to which the universal concept relates is initially distinct, but it must also remain distinct. According to this passage, a loving relationship cannot lapse into a night in which all cows are black.

These rather abstract themes will make their way into Hegel's discussion of ethical love in the *Philosophy of Right.* As I put it above, ethical love for Hegel is constituted by an interpersonal intimate relationship. Albeit a species of love in general, ethical love as I understand it will include elements that may not hold for love in all of its forms. For one, it is clear from Hegel's discussion that I can only ethically love another living human being, which would exclude pets and artefacts. For another, I can only ethically love another living human being who stands to me in a certain relation, ideally reciprocating my love. Ethical love cannot be one-sided, unrequited, although presumably other forms of love can. Perhaps I could continue to love a deceased spouse in the ethical sense, but not someone I never met. And perhaps I could ethically love a child, since Hegel will go on to describe the child as an expression of the love between two adults. Moreover, ethical love bears a close tie to recognition of another's singular individuality, for what I love in another when I love them ethically is their singular individuality. If we recall Antigone's recognition of her brother as *this brother*, Hegel is here suggesting that ethical love must hold itself to the same high

---

[93] *Science of Logic* 12:35, Giovanni translation p. 532.

standard, though its basis is no longer blood ties or non-erotic bonds. Rather, ethical love is a way of recognizing the singular individuality in the other, as well as in oneself, and in the connection between us. This is what distinguishes ancient marriages, which Hegel associates with the fulfillment of generic functions, from modern marriages, which have ethical love as their basis.

In formal terms, Hegel emphasizes that ethical love displays the structure of love in general, because it unifies separate elements, thereby giving rise to a new entity, the loving couple. This makes ethical love generative, for it creates something that did not previously exist, something that becomes irreducible and irresolvable into its parts. Such a process of unification presupposes a separation among the elements that are to be united, but it also overcomes their separation in some sense while at the same time preserving it in another sense. In order to avoid lapsing into a night in which all cows are black, differences must be actively sustained. Hegel claims that this makes love seemingly paradoxical, for is a process that must overcome difference and preserve difference, which may appear to be conflicting demands. He thus famously calls love "the most immense contradiction" (§158A), adding that ethical love is "both the production and resolution of this contradiction" (PR §158A). It raises the question of how ethical love can resolve this contradiction that (as a species of love in general) it invariably produces.

What I want to propose is that ethical love is supposed to be achieved through *cognition*, or what Hegel calls "consciousness." Hegel writes,

> Love means in general the *consciousness* of my unity with another, so that I am not isolated on my own for myself, but gain my *self-consciousness* only through the renunciation of my independent existence and through *knowing* myself as the unity of myself with another and of the other with me." (PR §158A, my emphasis)

Ethical love involves knowing these three distinct elements – myself, the other, and our relationship – as well as knowing *that* they are distinct yet related. By entering into a relationship, I both express and uncover aspects of myself of which I might have otherwise remained oblivious. This makes relationships an occasion for achieving self-knowledge. If I also know that it is in virtue of this relationship that I am able to both be and know myself in these distinct ways, to know myself as the unity of myself with another. Hegel's account is intended to caution against the fantasy that I can only become a singular individual and can only know myself as a singular individual if I avoid entering into intimate interpersonal relationships.

Hegel thinks I should welcome the constraints that relationships impose, because these constraints can give my life a determinate shape, making me into someone in particular. But I do not automatically maintain my awareness of myself as a distinct participant in the relationship in virtue of participating in these relationships. It is indeed possible to become absorbed by a relationship so as to grow unreal to oneself, a mere object of another's interpretation or a mere token to a type. What I just said about myself must also hold for the other. In short, I must know the other through this unity, which means that I must know the other as a singular individual, and as someone who is no less capable of adopting a take on our relationship. Iris Murdoch wrote that "love is the extremely difficult realization that something other than oneself is real" and that "love is the imaginative recognition of, that is respect for, this otherness."[94] These remarks should lead us to think that just as I can grow unreal to myself, so can the other person.[95]

As if this all were not complicated enough, ethical love also requires that I know the relationship itself, the connection between us, as a unity that is constituted by us but also independent of us. It is through such cognition that ethical love becomes *intelligent*, sensitively tracking the unfolding life of a relationship. It is possible to misinterpret a relationship, or to remain stuck with an obsolete interpretation of it. What makes cognizing the relationship itself so central is that the relationship is the very thing that singles out the individuals, giving them a determinate shape. One way to think about this would be to notice that, while there can be an indefinite series of people who have my spouses' charm, what makes my spouse singular in my eyes is the fact that I am married to this person and not to any of these others. As Niko Kolodny has argued, it seems strange to say that we love people for their qualities. Rather, "one's reasons for loving a person is one's relationship to her: the ongoing history one shares with her."[96] While this does not mean that what I love is our relationship instead of the other person, it does mean that my sense of our relationship informs when I take my ethical love to be appropriately directed at another. Ethical love is not to be conflated with falling in love, for loving someone in this ethical sense is loving them in virtue of a relationship that is already in place, rather than in virtue of what in another might be a source of my attraction to them.[97] But Hegel's account also brings into focus the self-regarding attitude that is implied by the value

---

[94] Murdoch, "The Sublime and the Good," 2015–2016, pp. 215–216.
[95] In "The Extremely Difficult Realization," Hopwood stresses that love for Murdoch must be directed at another's individuality. Hopwood also ascribes to Murdoch the following explanation for our tendency toward self-serving fantasy: "Faced with an object that cannot be fully possessed or assimilated, the ego creates for itself an object that *can* be possessed – a dream image or fantasy that gradually comes to substitute for the real person" (p. 491).
[96] Kolodny, "Love as Valuing a Relationship," pp. 135–136.
[97] "Although a person's qualities may serve as reasons for wanting, as well as seeking to cultivate, a friendship or romantic relationship with that person, they are not reasons for the attitude of friendship or romantic love that sustains the relationship once it is cultivated" (Kolodny, "Love as Valuing a Relationship," p. 140).

I place on a relationship. When I love another in virtue of our relationship, my love for another is also a love of that which binds us, and hence also a love for myself as a distinct participant in that union.[98]

Hegel would say that it is through cognition that ethical love prevents these elements from collapsing into an undifferentiated mass, which he spells out in terms of self-feeling and self-consciousness. Ethical love is supposed to be a family's "feeling [*Empfindung*] of its own unity" (PR §158), by which I take him to be saying that love is a feeling that any family member has of a unity of which they are a part. Feeling this unity can in principle coexist with feeling indifferent, frustrated, resentful toward a family member, but if I have negative feelings on a regular basis, these might be telling me that my relationships are no longer instances of ethical love. In his section on Subjective Spirit of the *Encyclopedia of the Philosophical Sciences*, Hegel advances a conception of self-feeling as an initial stage of self-awareness. Self-feeling can differentiate the material provided by particular feelings, preferring some of it to others, identifying with some of it at the exclusion of others.[99] Although these particular feelings can range from complex emotions to brute sensations, Hegel clears space for intelligent feelings, feelings that are responsive to that which provoked them. But self-feeling would nevertheless be insufficient for the cognition that ethical love requires. For one, self-feeling lacks the criteria by which to determine whether the particular feelings that emerge in response to objects are revealing something true about the objects that provoked them. For another, self-feeling does not yet relate to objects as genuinely independent, but only as prompts for my feelings. This makes self-feeling ultimately too self-regarding: I am monitoring how I feel and whether I can identify with my feelings, but I am not yet granting that which is provoking my feelings an independent reality.

It is for this reason that Hegel describes ethical love as also *self-conscious* love, which is supposed to surpass the inchoate intelligence of which self-feeling is capable. In order to evaluate whether I really am a part of a genuinely loving relationship, I need to become self-conscious of this relationship, an attitude that includes consciousness toward this relationship and toward those to whom I stand in this relationship. The notion of self-conscious love can conjure the image of someone who is perpetually thinking about the relationship, perhaps someone who is asking themselves why they love this person and whether they should

---

[98] Simon May, *Love,* has criticized Kolodny for placing too much emphasis on relationships. According to May, Kolodny cannot distinguish between loving and nonloving relationships, since to love just is to value an existing relationship. Also, May thinks that Kolodny does not allow for unrequited and unrequitable love, which May argues may be love in its most genuine form (p. 92). Independently of the question of Kolodny is offering a persuasive account of love in general, it is an illuminating account of "ethical love" in particular.

[99] Hegel thinks that self-feeling can lead to madness, citing romantic obsessions as an example.

continue loving them. Hegel would consider people plagued by such thoughts to be supremely alienated, hardly exemplars of ethical love. Instead, self-consciousness is supposed to be woven into the ways in which we inhabit a loving relationship. For Hegel, self-conscious love is manifested in "love, trust, and a sharing of the whole of individual existence" (PR §163). But Hegel nevertheless thinks that self-consciousness goes beyond self-feeling and is not automatically guaranteed by it. In other words, I could be feeling a unity of which I am part, and yet fail to be conscious of this unity. Instead, both consciousness and self-consciousness are properly speaking active accomplishments.

Marriage

So far, I have attempted to isolate ethical love, even though Hegel takes marriage to be the institutional home at which ethical love resides, defining marriage as *rightful ethical love* [*rechtliche sittliche Liebe*] (PR §161A). To put my cards on the table, I do not think that Hegel could be arguing that marriage is necessary or sufficient for ethical love, at most that it is conducive to its realization.[100] Marriage surpasses and thereby *fosters* and *fortifies* ethical love because it introduces an institutional framework. It is well known that Hegel rejects Kant's contractual model, according to which marriage is a "union of two persons of different sexes for lifelong possession of each other's sexual attributes."[101] Hegel dismisses this view as crude, not because it reduces marriage to sex, but because it reduces it to contract. On such a view, "marriage gives contractual form to the arbitrary relations between individuals, and is thus debased to a contract entitling the parties concerned to use one another" (PR §161A). For Hegel it is indeed important that marriage begin as a contract between two independent persons, as a "free consent" and "free surrender."[102] If either party were coerced into getting married, it would be hard to see how their eventual union could count as a free relation.[103] But Hegel thinks that marriage only begins in a contract; its aim is to overcome this contract.[104] When two people get married, both parties agree to

---

[100] According to Brake, marriage is neither necessary nor sufficient for the subjective transformation often associated with it, in virtue of which marriage is supposed to be an ethical (in her terminology *moral*) institution. Hegel is not saying that it is necessary or sufficient, only that this subjective transformation is an ideal that belongs to marriage as a concept.

[101] Kant takes sex to be in principle objectifying, so it can only become morally permissible (in conformity with the formula of humanity) in the context of marriage.

[102] According to Hegel, marriage in its "objective origin is the free consent of the persons concerned, and in particular their consent to *constitute a single person* and to give up their natural and individual personalities within this union" (PR §162).

[103] Even arranged marriages could be based on free consent and free surrender, as long as the individuals involved deliberately agree to heed parental guidance.

[104] Zdravko Kobe ("Keine Frau muss müssen?") develops a Hegelian notion of sexual consent through Hegel's critique of Kantian marriage.

become a "single person," which represents a unity that can no longer be grasped as an agreement between independent persons. A married couple as a couple becomes an entity that can own property, sign contracts, earn an income.[105]

Hegel also takes it to be significant that the marital contract be sealed in public in order to win the recognition from the broader community. It is for this reason that he emphasizes the importance of the wedding ceremony. In order for a marriage to assume a rightful status, there should be "the solemn declaration of consent to the ethical bond of marriage and its recognition and confirmation by the family and community" (PR §164). The bond between two people becomes actual and ethical not just through a ceremony that other people witness, but also through its expression in language. This means that unlike informal forms of ethical love, which may emerge gradually, a marriage begins at an identifiable moment in time as a public event of two people making a verbal promise to one another. We can date the start of a marriage in a way in which we may not be able to date the start of other intimate interpersonal relationships. For Hegel, this moment in time makes clear that ethical love brings something new into existence, something that did not precede the ceremony. In this way, Hegel's position parts not only with those who saw the wedding as superfluous, but also those who see marriage as having no specific beginning in time. Stanley Cavell has entertained the possibility that getting married may be a repetitive act, for "only those can genuinely marry who are already married. It is as though you know you are married when you come to see that you cannot divorce, that is, when you find that your lives simply will not disentangle."[106] Hegel would want to distinguish between a discovery made before and a discovery made after a ceremony, since he would deny that people can discover that they are already married before they have participated in this ceremony.

Marriage can also be described as a "transformative choice" (borrowing L. A. Paul's terminology), namely, a big life decision that will lead you down a path that exceeds what you can anticipate.[107] Hegel thinks that what makes the decision to get married transformative is its comprehensive commitment, for

---

[105] Carole Pateman argues that Hegel's view of marriage is incoherent, because it presupposes that women can enter into contracts while denying them the relevant capacities, and because it assumes that two can become one person without the one party (women) becoming erased for the personhood of another (men). See Pateman, "Marriage and the Standpoint of Contract." In "No Utopia," I have argued that Hegel does not think that the personhood of women is erased by marriage while that of men is preserved, but that he thinks wives become members of a single person – the couple – that is merely "represented" by the husband as head.

[106] Cavell, *Pursuits of Happiness,* p. 126. The contrast Cavell draws might presuppose courting rituals that would have been foreign to Hegel. Cavell's question is not exactly what counts as undergoing a wedding ceremony, but what makes a marriage real or valid even after the ceremony.

[107] L. A. Paul, *Transformative Experience*. Her primary example is becoming a parent.

marriage is only justifiable as an institution if the interactions between spouses do not resemble transactions, two people running a household in the way they may manage a business. Marriage cannot become yet another form of negotiation. The comprehensive nature of its commitment implies that you are now enlisted in a collective endeavor that takes incontestable precedence over all other projects. Hegel frames this collective endeavor as the "sharing of a life." We might wonder whether this requirement is already built into the concept of ethical love, or whether it first emerges with the concept of marriage. In any case, the way in which this requirement is conventionally interpreted is as a commitment to spending life together "until death do you part," to sexual exclusivity, maybe even to reproducing life through offspring. Hegel is definitely not contesting these conventional interpretations of marriage, but I want to flag that the requirement itself is indeterminate. It does not imply a specific duration in time, or a specific object of common concern. We can also in principle imagine consecutive relationships that last for limited periods of time or even multiple overlapping relationships, though polyamory would stretch Hegel's view very far. Not only does Hegel explicitly characterize marriage as dyadic and monogamous (PR §167), but he also worries about dissolving ethical love into associations of convenience, viable only so long as they support my individual projects.

So far, I have focused on the aspects of marriage that Hegel takes to be conducive to the realization of ethical love. But Hegel also provides a few reasons, perhaps hidden in his text, for worrying that marriage actually obstructs the realization of ethical love.[108] In his early fragment on love, Hegel wrote that lovers are to see each other as thoroughly alive. One way to understand this would be to say that it requires being open to the possibility that the other will continue to surprise me no matter how well I have come to know them. And you might suspect that marriage is going to be marred by the habit it tends to produce. Hegel himself espouses an ambivalent assessment of habit, arguing that habit both enlivens and deadens. On the one hand, "[f]amiliarity, acquaintance, and the habit of shared activity should not be present before marriage: they should be discovered only within it, and the value of this discovery is all the greater the richer it is and the more components it has" (PR §168A). On the other hand,

> Human beings even die as a result of habit – that is, if they have become totally habituated to life ... For they are active only in so far as they have not yet attained something and wish to assert themselves and show what they can do in pursuit of it. Once this is accomplished, their activity and vitality disappear, and the loss of interest which ensues is mental and physical death. (PR §151A)

---

[108] Adrian Daub describes this as the "problem of the product," namely, that the relationship that is supposed to become a realization of ethical love becomes an "ossified third term" (Daub, *Uncivil Unions*, p. 35).

In effect, habitual ways of relating to one another also can make us inattentive to changes in what we are used to seeing, which can impair the consciousness that married people have of themselves, of one another, and of their relationship.[109] It is the habit of sharing a life that allows ethical love to strike root, but it is this same habit that also threatens ethical love as an ongoing form of cognition of that which is living.[110]

In his early fragment on love, Hegel also claimed that love requires equality. This is perhaps marriage's greatest hurdle.[111] It is worth keeping in mind that Hegel rejects abstract interpretations of equality, according to which equality demands quantitative or qualitative sameness incompatible with internal differentiation or functional specialization.[112] He would say that marriage as a joint endeavor is only possible if its participants are willing to assume different roles to maintain the life of the couple.[113] As long as a marriage is going well, these roles will not be experienced as sacrifices or as burdens. It is only when a marriage begins to crumble that there is a reckoning with whatever differences were present in it, a taking stock of who was obliged to do what and who was permitted to do what, of who was bearing the brunt for keeping the relationship going. The fact that gender settles many of these questions in advance (not just for Hegel, but also for us) makes it all the more vivid that living with inequality may be the price that marriage extracts. Of course, Hegel himself fully embraces a picture of marriage as a heterosexual and patriarchal institution. It also happens to be a picture that corresponds to his social milieu, a context in which differentiated gender roles were becoming increasingly pronounced.[114] This makes it difficult to see how Hegel can claim that marriage preserves

---

[109] For more on the connection between habit and knowledge, see my *Hegel on Second Nature in Ethical Life*.

[110] This would be one example of taking "living" to refer not only to natural organisms, but to logical structure that can be instantiated by social phenomena as well.

[111] For an in-depth discussion of the question of marriage and equality, see Gal Katz's "Love is between living beings." Katz argues that Hegel thinks a marriage could be internally equal even if it is externally hierarchical.

[112] That realization requires differentiation is already clear from Hegel's characterization of the "universal concept" (in the *Science of Logic*) as akin to 'free love' because it necessarily includes internal differences.

[113] "Whenever Hegel understands some social function to be necessary to a form of life's continuance and maintenance, he tends to look for discrete job-holders for those functions" (Pinkard, *Hegel's Phenomenology*, p. 306).

[114] See Hausen, "Die Polarisierung," in particular her analysis of lexicons and similar texts, which articulated these conceptual resources. She analyzes the emergence of these gender differences as both the consequence of the gendered division of labor and a means for ideologically justifying this division, warning bourgeois women against seeking work outside their homes. Her analysis also shows that Hegel's conceptual distinctions between universality and individuality, as well as thinking and feeling, as applied to sexual difference were widespread in the discourse of his time.

equality. As Jean Bethke Elshtain has put it, "Like the inhabitants of Orwell's *Animal Farm* who learn that all animals are created equal but some are more equal than others, the inhabitants of Hegel's conceptual universe are ethically significant but some are more significant than others."[115] This would mean that to enter into marriage along Hegel's preferred lines would be to learn the lesson that although both individuals are to be liberated by marriage, not everyone's liberation is of equal value.[116]

This impression is not wholly off the mark, for Hegel clearly welcomes the fact that this reciprocal liberation will mean different things for men and for women. In a significant passage, Hegel writes, "The natural determinacy of the two sexes acquires an intellectual and ethical significance by virtue of its rationality. This significance is determined by the difference into which the ethical substantiality, as the concept in itself, divides itself up in order that its vitality may thereby achieve a concrete unity" (PR ¶165). This feature of Hegel's argument seems on the face of it to violate his conclusions in his chapter from the *Phenomenology of Spirit*, in which he criticizes ancient ethical life for relying on natural considerations in assigning social roles.[117] It could look as if Hegel were appealing to nature in an illegitimate way in order to argue that marriage must be between men and women and that men and women must perform distinct tasks.[118] As I read him, Hegel is appealing to nature, but in a circuitous way, for he is arguing that sexual difference is rational because it promotes ethical love. If ethical love is a process of unification of that which is initially divided, it presupposes a preceding basis for differentiation, and hence benefits from whatever differences it happens to find (in nature).[119] I am also struck by the fact that Hegel offers a social (intellectual and ethical) interpretation of sexual difference, which he concedes is amplified through education (PR §166A).[120]

---

[115] Elshtain, *Public Man, Private Woman*, p. 174. Elshtain's point is that "man is the public being and woman is the private being" (p. 180), and Hegel ranks the public sphere above the private sphere.

[116] Some commentators have pointed out that women lose their equal *legal* standing: "The legal status of marriage, indeed, takes on a peculiarly oppressive character, granted that one of the parties, the woman, is not herself permitted to enter the legal domain in her own right" (Joanna Hodge, p. 132).

[117] Ravven, "Has Hegel Anything to Say to Feminists?" argues that Hegel criticizes the ancient family for being unreflective, undifferentiated, and relying on natural harmony, and that these are the same reasons to criticize the modern family.

[118] Deranty accuses Hegel of making this mistake (p. 156). According to Stone, "We may still think that Hegel's particular argument for women's place in the family makes illegitimate reference to mere nature. For presumably the reason why women and not men are deemed to be the rightful representatives of the family sphere is because of women's reproductive biology and functions" (Stone, "Gender, the Family, and the Organic State," p. 154).

[119] Brauer in *Natur* und *Sittlichkeit* argues that sexual difference is special among natural differences because Hegel takes it to be of the highest order (p. 141).

[120] Susanne Lettow has suggested that Hegel has no space for a sex-gender distinction, because he derives gender from reproductive differences in nature. I agree that the space is slim, but I also

Given that Hegel thinks of ethical love as an ongoing form of cognition, it is unsurprising that he goes on to emphasize the differences between men and women in cognitive terms. Hegel claims that men can know and will universal ends (through conceptual thought), whereas women can know and will concrete individuals (though feeling). Here Hegel is admittedly appealing to sexist stereotypes about thinking and feeling. But his broader point is that each mode is on its own insufficient to yield cognition in any full sense of the term, which suggests that men and women must cooperate in an overarching process of cognition.[121] The difference between feeling and thinking is also supposed to undergird a gendered division of labor, explaining why men and women are equipped (by nature) to perform different tasks. Since women are supposedly more affectively attentive to individuals, he concludes that they turn out to be better suited for care work. And since men supposedly think about universal purposes, he concludes that they turn out to be better suited for professional and political roles.

Hegel offers the following description of this gendered division of labor:

> Man there has his actual substantial life in the state, in learning [*Wissenschaft*] and such, and otherwise in work and struggle with the external world and with himself, so that it is only through his division [*Entzweiung*] that he fights his way to self-sufficient unity with himself. In the family, he has a peaceful intuition of this unity, and an emotive and subjective ethical life. Woman, however, has her substantial vocation in the family, and her ethical disposition consists in this piety. (PR §166)

As Terry Pinkard has put it, Hegel wants to show that "the patriarchal bourgeois family therefore has things just right. The woman is sovereign over the household (the realm of caring), and the man is the breadwinner (in the market, the realm of struggle and competition)."[122] This patriarchal bourgeois family has it "just right" because it has assigned the right individual to the right job, making the best use of what nature has provided. But you might think that the patriarchal bourgeois family has gotten it very wrong, because it deforms individual as knowers, thwarting the development of those cognitive capacities that each of them would need in order to achieve ethical love. If each spouse is only cultivating one capacity at the expense of others, you might think that neither of them will be capable of truly cognizing themselves, each other, and the unity of which they are a part.

---

think that Hegel does not simply reduce the ethical meaning of sexual difference to its natural meaning. At the very least, we can say that that the natural underdetermines the ethical.

[121] This insufficiency is clearer in the second case, that one would have to know both universal purposes and be able to recognize them as realized in singular contexts in order to count as knowing in the full sense. But you might also think that knowing is going to include an affective dimension, which would make feeling relevant to thinking.

[122] Pinkard, *Hegel's Phenomenology*, p. 306.

Hegel's picture of the gendered division of labor is undeniably stark. Although we might be tempted to dismiss Hegel for betraying his own requirement of equality, it is worth acknowledging that Hegel thinks he is describing an egalitarian form of marriage. He takes his insistence on the need for free consent, and on the need of a wedding ceremony, to be institutional ways of protecting women's rights.[123] In his marginalia, Hegel even writes that one ought to respect and place women as equal to oneself ("*die Frau als sich gleich achten and setzen*") and that men should not count for more than women ("*Mann soll nicht mehr gelten als die Frau*").[124] Given that both care work and other work maintain a marriage and the nuclear family to which it gives rise, Hegel could in principle have concluded that men and women make equally valuable contributions to this collective endeavor in which they are both enlisted.[125] Maybe Hegel believed that this was already his view. But then we can ask ourselves whether the problem lies in the fact that care work is insufficiently or inadequately valued, and we can also wonder whether we should suppose that liberation is only possible through participation in the workforce.[126] However it is that the institution of marriage could or should be reformed, or whether it should just be abolished, what Hegel takes to be truly valuable about marriage is not the institution per se, but the ethical love to which it aspires, and which it so often (perhaps unavoidably) betrays.

4 Parents and Children

"It is not the having of children that turns us into slaves: it is not the son that enslaves us, but the father.

-Carla Lonzi, "Let's Spit on Hegel"

Dissolving the Family

Children can be seen as the main obstacle to imagining a future without families, since families provide the prime contexts in which children are brought into the

---

[123] Behind Hegel's comment about seducers (in his criticism of *Lucinde*) is his worry that seducers were harmful to women because they can leave them without the "honor" and the legal safety of marriage.

[124] *Philosophie des Rechts,* Suhrkamp, Volume 7, §167, p. 321. In these notes, Hegel is comparing modern marriage favorably to chivalry and polygamy. He thinks that in the case of chivalry, women were placed above men, and in the case of polygamy, they were placed below men.

[125] See Moyar's discussion of the family in *Hegel's Value*. Moyar writes, "The challenge is to settle on what activities count for what, and in particular to recognize the value of childrearing without having to go to court in a divorce settlement" (p. 220).

[126] Stafford in "The Feminist Critique of Hegel" argues that Hegel's position clarifies the limits of liberal individualism and the assumption that the liberation of women must take the form of professional self-actualization. Landes makes a similar point: "the modern critic of Hegel's theory of the family must confront the fundamental issue he poses for those who would offer a vision of equality and liberation that remain trapped within the limits of egoistic individualism" ("Hegel's Conception of the Family," p. 27).

world and raised into adults. Even though not everyone becomes a parent, nearly everyone has parents. When we compare the three relationships with which we began, that between parent and child will look to be the least contingent, because it is the least dependent on the existence of social institutions. We might even picture families as clusters of relationships that congeal around children: while these relations themselves can shift and change, children remain their inflexible foundation. Until now, I have underplayed the role of offspring in Hegel's account of the modern family. I wanted to emphasize that Hegel's argument does not take children as its starting point, at least not insofar as children are assumed to be a fact of life that must be accommodated in one way or another. That said, children make an important contribution to Hegel's concept of the family, for it is only through children that we can come to think of the family as a transgenerational person with recourse to material resources [*Vermögen*], usually known as family inheritance. So, it is through children that the material aspect of the family, as well as the family as a property-owning entity, first comes into view. Hegel even foregrounds this association between children and resources, claiming that they are two different ways in which the unity of the family is exhibited.

We can see that Hegel does not take children as his starting point by considering their place in his argument in favor of the nuclear family. Hegel claims that a married couple is sufficient to count as a nuclear family, whether or not it produces children (PR §172).[127] Hegel also does not conflate the biological "imperative" that there be children for the sake of the species with an ethical imperative to procreate.[128] Instead, he thinks he needs to provide a reason to have children; the fact that doing so also contributes to the species is at most an added benefit.[129] The reason he suggests is that ethical love is incomplete without children: "the relationship of love is not yet objective between man and woman – for while their substantial unity exists in feeling [*Empfindung*], it still lacks objectivity. Parents obtain such objectivity only in children" (PR §173A). One way to make sense of this would be to say that a relationship of ethical love remains elusive if it hinges solely on the attitudes of the people involved, if it lives primarily in the minds of spouses so-to-speak, in their self-feeling and self-consciousness. Rather, ethical love becomes something with a life of its own, something that cannot simply dissipate into thin air,

---

[127] Hegel rejects the view of marriage that comes from the natural law tradition, according to which the good of marriage is procreation. Although Hegel will not deny that marriage also has such purposes to fulfill, he thinks that this view reduces marriage to its "physical aspect" or "natural character" (PR §161A).

[128] I am grateful to Karen Ng for conversations about this topic.

[129] The fact that Hegel thinks he needs to provide people with a reason to have children shows just how modern his position is. For an analysis of contemporary deliberations around whether to have children, see Anastasia Berg and Rachel Wiseman's *What Are Children For?*

when it takes on an independent existence, paradigmatically in children, who become the embodiments of ethical love.[130] A specific child is both the object of ethical love and the medium through which ethical love is expressed, for "in the child, the mother loves the husband and he his wife; in it, they see their love before them" (PR §173A). With the child, the nuclear family is complete.[131] The requirement that there be a child in order to complete the family also shows that the nuclear family is never a completely self-enclosed unit – it always points beyond its own borders.[132]

Hegel's chapter on the family concludes with children, devoting its final section to childrearing [*Erziehung*], which is also a section devoted to the dissolution of the family, both the ethical and the natural disintegration from one into many. In short, by having children, you are producing more singular individuals who will ideally go on to form families of their own, thus preserving the institution of the family by extending it indefinitely into the future. From the family's own distinct perspective, a perspective that is not to be conflated with that of nature, children serve as the vehicles for the perpetuation of family, rather than the family serving as the vehicle for children – or at least it is hard to say which is the chicken and which the egg.[133] But the task of childrearing is primarily that of creating singular individuals who become capable of entering into free relationships, which means that they must first separate from their family of origin before they can form a new family. Moreover, Hegel stresses that childrearing cannot happen in a vacuum. He recounts the anecdote concerning a Pythagorean, who when asked how one is to educate a son in ethical matters, replied: "Make him a citizen of a state with good laws" (PR §153). Note that this anecdote refers to sons, not to daughters. A daughter never leaves the family, even temporarily, for her vocation is exhausted by her participation in it.

In this third and final section, I will explore the parent–child relationship through the lens of sexual difference. If we return to the gender roles we saw in

---

[130] As Thimo Heisenberg points out in "Hegel on Childless Marriage," this is a neglected aspect of Hegel's argument, usually dismissed as yet another outdated claim. Heisenberg defends Hegel as expressing a "grain of truth," namely, "that a committed love relationship comes with a *general social requirement:* to truly care about one another as a couple, we also have to jointly care about somebody else."

[131] You might accept that spousal love requires an independent object and yet question whether this object needs to be a child, or a biologically related child. What speaks in favor of childrearing in particular is that children kill two birds with one stone: they objectify marital love, and they also perpetuate the species. This makes them an especially appropriate way of completing a family. On Hegel's silence on adoption, see Brauer, pp. 148–149.

[132] Brake discusses alternative marital ceremonies during which people commit themselves as a couple to aesthetic, intellectual, or political pursuits.

[133] "From the point of view of nature, the presupposition of persons existing immediately – as parents – here becomes the result, a process which runs on into the infinite progression of generations which produce and presuppose one another" (PR §173).

marriage, we might assume that Hegel is drawing on men and women's reproductive capabilities, specifically their supposed activity and inactivity, in order to derive conclusions about the social roles to which they are "naturally" suited. While this does not quite capture Hegel's line of thinking, motherhood and fatherhood do represent two sets of tasks that give rise to two different kinds of relationships to the child. Starting with motherhood, I will examine how Hegel conceives of pregnancy and what conclusions we can draw, specifically for the nature of childrearing. In his "Anthropology," Hegel mentions pregnant women as examples of what he calls "genius," which is an immediate form of knowing. I will argue that this picture of pregnancy promises a different avenue for thinking about motherhood in Hegel's account of the family and suggests another place at which Hegel casts the family as a site of learning.

Turning next to fatherhood, I will examine Hegel's conception of a family's material resources, which the male "head" of the family would have been tasked to procure and administer. You might think that Hegel's references to material resources is the clearest indicator that Hegel thinks of the family as a private unit, a person across time that owns private property with which those who are not members of this family cannot meddle. But Hegel distinguishes between property [*Eigentum*] on the one hand, and assets [*Vermögen*] on the other. While Hegel argues that only individual persons can own property, he does allow for the possibility that material resources can be collectively owned, hence owned by groups of people whose borders are at least potentially open-ended. Hegel's concept of material resources thus suggests a way of combusting the parent–child relationship, making it far less self-contained. We might even think that it points to a path away from families as privatized sources of care.

Childbearing and Childrearing

Recall that Hegel seeks to justify sexual difference in the institution of marriage by claiming that it is a lucky accident of nature that it generates a separation for ethical love to overcome. Since we can imagine nature producing other lucky accidents of the same kind, Hegel's justification does not show sexual difference to be necessary to ethical love. Once children enter into the picture, however, sexual difference assumes an additional significance, since it also happens to enable biological reproduction. In the *Philosophy of Right*, Hegel mentions biological reproduction only in passing. It is really in the *Philosophy of Nature*, specifically in the lecture notes, where Hegel discusses the relevantly reproductive capacities between males and females more extensively.[134] So with the parent–child relation, we

---

[134] Encyclopedia II, §369Z. Sexual difference is not mentioned in the main paragraph.

arrive at the vexed question of whether (and if so, how) to read the *Philosophy of Right* and the *Philosophy of Nature* alongside each other. As Alison Stone has put it, "Clearly, Hegel understood his account of reproduction in those paragraphs to identify and explain the distinct nature of the two sexes and so to provide a basis for his sociopolitical division of gender roles."[135] I am inclined to think that while it is surely a good idea to look at what Hegel says about males and females in his *Philosophy of Nature,* we should not expect that it will identify, explain, or ground what he goes on to say about men and women in the *Philosophy of Right*.

The *Philosophy of Nature* argues for three claims that will be worth keeping in mind. First, Hegel holds that a species itself is neither male nor female, which makes sexual difference an internal differentiation within a species, rendering masculinity and femininity variations on a common type. Second, Hegel assumes that we can draw structural comparisons between male and female reproductive organs. For example, he asks what the male equivalent of the uterus would be: the prostates, the gland? Or is it that the labia are the female equivalent of the prostate? Third, Hegel suggests that what makes these variations nonetheless different is that the female version represents an "undifferentiated unity" that Hegel interprets as inactive (*untätig*), whereas the male represents "division" and "opposition" that Hegel interprets as active (*tätig*).[136] He points to the movement of blood as a basis for distinguishing males and females along these lines: menstruation is the loss of blood, hence a form of inactivity, whereas the penis swells with blood, hence an example of activity.[137] Hegel concludes that the clitoris must be *inactive feeling in general*.

Although the details of his analysis are easy to ridicule, they indicate that Hegel thinks of sexual difference in nature as a matter of *hierarchical complementarity*. The reproductive organs of males and females are different and compatible, plus they can be ranked as higher and lower, depending on whether they are active or inactive. Many have turned to these comments in order to show that Hegel is reiterating the same point in his account of marriage, in which Hegel describes men as like animals (hence active) and women as like plants (hence inactive, or passive).[138] But it is far from clear what his reflections on biological reproduction are supposed to yield, what bearing they have on

---

[135] Stone, "Sexual Polarity in Schelling and Hegel," p. 267

[136] As Stone points out, Hegel treats the female as the privation of masculinity (inactive), rather than as a positive in her own right (passive) ("Sexual Polarity," p. 260).

[137] Even here, Hegel is again seeking analogies, comparisons, or correspondences: "[T]his male blood filling [Bluterfuellung] thus correspond to the female bleeding [Bluterguss]" (Encyclopedia II, §369Z).

[138] Note that animals and plants also do not obviously complement or complete each other.

Hegel's views about men and women.[139] Susanne Brauer has already exposed the weaknesses in any argument available to Hegel that attempts to explain social differences in terms of these putative natural differences. First, if Hegel were claiming that women are inactive because their clitoris is inactive, he would be confusing a part for a whole.[140] Second, Hegel could not be deriving social differences from natural differences without falling prey to circular reasoning, since his basis for interpreting reproductive organs as either active or passive are his background assumptions about social gender roles.[141] Third, the active-passive distinction is only one difference mentioned in his *Philosophy of Right*, which includes many more differences between men and women that cannot be derived from it. As we have seen, Hegel describes men and women as cultivating different cognitive skills, with men oriented toward universal purposes and women oriented toward individuals. This distinction between universal and individual does not have anything obviously to do with activity and inactivity.

But my main reason for hesitation is Hegel's own conception of pregnancy, specifically human pregnancy, which Hegel intimates in his "Anthropology." This conception of pregnancy appears in his section on the feeling soul, specifically in the context of what Hegel calls a "genius," which he takes to be a relational concept. To be a "genius" in Hegel's sense is to be a genius in relation to another self, but a self that is not yet fully formed and for this reason powerless to resist the genius' "magical" influence. Note that no one is a genius without qualification – people can only be *another*'s genius. His prime example is a pregnant woman's relation to the fetus. As Hegel puts it, "The mother is the *genius* of the child, because by genius one usually means the selfish totality of spirit insofar as it exists for itself and constitutes the subjective substantiality of another, which is only externally determined as an individual."[142] Hegel's point is that a fetus can be considered an individual only to an observer, since a fetus has not yet undergone the process of individuating itself. Hegel describes the connection that a pregnant woman bears to the fetus as "psychic" because it is a mixture of the corporeal or material, as well as the spiritual or mental. His example of such a magical influence is that of a pregnant woman who has broken her arm, or who fears that she may have broken her arm, and who gives birth to a child with a damaged arm.[143] Hegel takes this example to display their

---

[139] See Easton: "Unlike the reductionist political theorists with whom he is often identified, Hegel distances his account of marriage and the family from approaches which focus on biological needs, which reduce the relationship between men and women to a natural biological basis" (p. 34).
[140] Brauer, p. 129. [141] See Brauer, pp. 128–129, and also p. 233.
[142] Encyclopedia III, §405R. [143] Encyclopedia III, §405A.

magical relation because it attests to an influence that cannot be reduced either to the corporeal or to the spiritual.

Hegel's conception of pregnancy as a relation of genius provides us with an alternative picture of the "feminine" in the reproductive process. While we should avoid trying to derive gender roles in the family from Hegel's "Anthropology," which would not be much better than trying to derive them from his *Philosophy of Nature,* Hegel's "anthropological" reflections nonetheless show that even if we focus solely on biological reproduction in the human case, Hegel does not see a mother as inactive. On the one hand, a mother carries her offspring within their own body, which means that she does not relate to it as to something different and distinct. On the other hand, Hegel also thinks that a mother can impact a fetus with her own mind, or her own soul, in a way that is similar to the influence exerted upon a medium in a séance. She has agency, even if her agency is limited, since the process of growing another human being exceeds what she can deliberately control. In Rachel Cusk's bleak words, "my communication with the baby always ends up taking the undignified form of my pleading with it not to hurt me. As my stomach grows bigger, I realize that getting in touch with it is about as useful as a field getting in touch with the motorway being built through it."[144] If we return to Hegel's distinction between the undifferentiated unity that he associated with femininity and the division or opposition that he associated with masculinity, we can see that pregnancy exemplifies a self-differentiation that cuts across this divide – you are literally splitting your single self into two selves, generating a different self out of yourself, and this other self is also participating in the process, differentiating itself gradually from all that surrounds it, primarily from you as its source.

This insight into self-differentiation as the anthropological basis of human life shows that Hegel did not forget that every human being comes out of the body of another and that this means that some human beings carry others inside their own.[145] If we pursue this process past the stage of pregnancy, we can see that self-differentiation shapes the role of motherhood into early childhood education. Although Hegel does not delve deeply into the mother–child relation in the *Philosophy of Right*, self-differentiation informs his account of childrearing, which would have been a mother's central task within the family. A bourgeois wife of Hegel's time was responsible primarily for providing and managing the education of children, rather than for the myriad chores (cooking, cleaning, etc.) that we associate with reproductive labor today. But Hegel would

---

[144] Rachel Cusk, *A Life's Work*.
[145] This is a criticism that Susan Okin Moller raises against many political theories, for instance Nozick's (see pp. 79–88). Easton describes Hegel's theory of the family to be a "living refutation of the state of nature" as a state of natural self-interest (p. 36).

have had to admit that mothering is itself a comparably demanding set of activities whose primary goal is to create the conditions under which this other inchoate self, the infant and toddler, can individuate. Because these conditions are so crucial for the emergence of singular individuality, Axel Honneth has taken the mother–child relationship (not the husband – wife relationship as Hegel himself) to be at the core of the family.[146] According to Honneth, it is the mother–child relationship that provides a paradigm for the kind of recognition that the family uniquely affords. Honneth draws on psychological research into the stage when a child begins to vent aggression against its mother, not because it is frustrated that the mother no longer meets its every need, but because it is testing its boundary from that which is not simply an extension of itself.[147] The sense of safety that a mother creates provides the backbone for all subsequent explorations.

As far as the tasks of childrearing are concerned, Hegel makes two points. First, children should enter into the feeling of unity that is characteristic of the family, so that they can develop the right affects (love and trust) that will serve them later in life. This makes producing and sustaining such a unity a prerequisite for early childhood development. Second, children also need to be expelled from their "natural determinacy," which Hegel thinks requires breaking their arbitrary will. We can think about this stage of development in relation to the achievement of singular individuality. In order that I become a singular individual capable of exceeding the demands of a social role, I need to cultivate a capacity for abstraction.[148] It would be reasonable to think that cultivating this capacity requires the use of means such as punishment and discipline, but Hegel emphasizes that these are to be employed only for the sake of realizing freedom, and not for some other sake. He states in no uncertain terms that children are not their parents' property – they are free "in themselves," which means that they are determined to become free, even if developing their potential for freedom takes considerable time and effort. In this vein, Hegel recommends rather strict methods of childrearing. For example, he advises against reasoning with children, since he thinks that giving a child reasons will only fortify this child's caprice (PR§174A). Although it is ultimately an empirical question which methods will be most effective, the very fact that methods are required shows that childrearing is work, and hence that

---

[146] As Honneth puts it, "the emergence, in the relation between mother and child, of the 'being oneself in another' ... represents the model for all more mature forms of love" (Honneth, *The Struggle for Recognition,* p. 100). This is in keeping with what Simon May describes as the recent advent of parental love as the new archetype of love in general.

[147] See Honneth's discussion of Winnicott, *Struggle for Recognition,* pp. 98–105.

[148] Hegel describes this as the 'indeterminacy of the will' (PR §5).

mothering is work. Turning infants and toddlers into free adults is hardly an "imperceptible plant-like unfolding," either on the child's or on the mother's side.[149] Pregnancy is only the beginning of this long labor of self-differentiation.[150]

It is worth pausing to consider why Hegel chose the term "genius" for this seemingly magical influence that a mother exerts over her child. It is well known that Hegel was not in favor of the more common concept of genius defined as a rare intelligence endowed by nature that you either have or don't.[151] But the fact that he calls pregnant women geniuses implies that he is not thinking of them as "mindless mothers" (to borrow Joanna Hodge's formulation), for a genius possesses what Hegel describes as an immediate form of knowledge.[152] Although Hegel is known as the "great foe of immediacy" (as Sellars so memorably put it), Hegel is in fact not wholly dismissive of immediate knowledge. A genius-mother would know immediately how to interact with her child, though not in virtue of her inborn nature, but in virtue of bearing and raising a child.[153] Hegel describes her knowledge as "immediate" not primarily because it is a practical know-how, but because he does not think it can be derived from observation or justified in terms of evidence. The analogy he draws is with the ability to see with your eyes closed, without recourse to sight or light.[154] A century later, Hegel's "genius-mother" resurfaced in the writings of the St. Louis Hegelian Susan Blow, who served as director of the first kindergarten program in the United States. Blow wanted to combine Hegel's conception of individual development with Froebel's pedagogical methods in order to put forward a program for kindergarten education that would draw on the immediate knowledge of genius-mothers. She made the case that professional educators have a lot to learn from mothers, and even more boldly, that motherhood should be seen as a trained profession in its own right.[155]

---

[149] "The education of women takes place imperceptibly, as if through the atmosphere of representational thought, more through living than through the acquisition of knowledge ... " (PR §166A).

[150] Scholz in "Hegel on Reproductive Labor" has argued that Hegel's conception of labor as externalization in which the worker comes to see himself in the object cannot be neatly applied to reproductive labor.

[151] For Hegel's critique of artistic genius, see Lydia Moland, *Hegel's Aesthetics,* pp. 47–51.

[152] Hodge, "Women and the Hegelian State," p. 151.

[153] Hegel takes séances and animal magnetism to be examples of it.

[154] As he puts it, "feeling or the subjective way of knowing, dispenses wholly, or at least in part, with the mediations and conditions indispensable to an objective knowledge and can, for example, perceive visible things without the aid of the eye or with the mediation of light" (Encyclopedia III, §406A).

[155] See Dorothy Rogers, *America's First Women Philosophers.* She describes Blow as "professionalizing motherhood" because Blow encouraged mothers to improve their methods and take classes (p. 62).

Material Resources

A child can be seen as the expression of ethical love, but it can also be seen as the heir of a family's assets.[156] The term that Hegel uses is *Vermögen*, which could also be translated as (material) resources. While "assets" indicates that Hegel is thinking of *Vermögen* as something that the family possesses, "resources" indicates that he is also thinking of it as something that enables, empowers.[157] In the following statement Hegel alludes to this association between children and assets: "Whereas [the unity of husband and wife] is present in their assets only as in an external thing, it is present in their children in a spiritual form" (PR ¶173A). Assets and children are cast as two different expressions of a marital union, though they turn out to be interconnected, because Hegel ultimately concludes that it is in virtue of children that a family needs assets in his sense. To have a child is to produce an individual that requires assets more than other family members do, because this child can only develop into a free being if its family has assets upon which to draw. As Hegel puts it, "[c]hildren have a right to be *brought up* and *supported* at the expense of the family" (PR ¶174), which means that a family must be in a position to bear this expense. Although Hegel does not specify the exact threshold for satisfying this right, he is conceding that childbearing and child-rearing have economic preconditions. Since Hegel thinks that it is the task of the male head of the household to procure and manage a family's assets, I want to suggest that the view of the child as heir is the perspective most closely aligned with fatherhood. I also want to suggest that it is not the child as such, but the child as heir, that presents the final obstacle to family abolition.

Hegel's discussion of a family's assets shows that Hegel is attempting to accommodate the intuition about the family with which we began, namely, that families are privatized sources of care that carry the heavy burden of meeting our most basic needs. These are not only the natural material needs for food and shelter; they are also our "spiritual" material needs. As David V. Ciavatta has put it, a "child assumes the reliability and familiarity of her family's things, and develops an enduring way of being in the world ... within the particular sphere of life opened up by these collective things."[158] In other words, in order to develop into free beings, children need not just a house, but a *home*, a space in which they feel at home. If we jump ahead to Hegel's chapter on "Civil

---

[156] Marina Martinez Mateo, *Kritik der Familie*, suggests that these two cannot be fully distinguished: "Die Liebe zum Kind ist die Liebe zum Erbe." This means either: *love for a child is love for an heir*, or *love for a child is love for inheritance*.

[157] Several commentators have pointed out the double meaning of *Vermögen*. See especially Bockenheimer, p. 267. Hodge translates it as "competence," p. 139.

[158] Ciavatta, *Spirit, the Family, and the Unconscious*, p. 184.

Society," we find that it is this feature of the family that makes it a form of "organized poverty" (to return to Sophie Lewis' expression), for it is this feature of the family that makes the poverty that civil society itself produces all the harder to endure. According to Hegel, the fact that our first family will in many cases fail to meet these basic needs gives rise to the demand for corporations, which have been compared to labor unions. Hegel refers to corporations as a "second family" because corporations have as their purpose "to protect its members against particular contingencies, and to educate others so as to make them eligible for membership" (PR §252). Since membership in corporations is selective, many will fall through their cracks. But the fact that Hegel is willing to call a corporation a *second family* shows that he acknowledges that a second family might be needed, and that he is willing to expand the term "family" beyond its usual connotations.

Hegel is well aware that the family's economic role has changed significantly over time. Premodern families were paradigmatically extended families that included many more members and so consisted of wider networks that could provide care in case one member fell upon hard times. This is no longer true of the nuclear family, which has shrunk to the size of parents and their children, with far less upon which to draw. Pre-modern families were also often engaged in collective forms of work, with children and other relatives contributing to, say, a family business or a family farm. This is also no longer true of the bourgeois family, which has singled out one individual from within its ranks as now solely responsible for accumulating a family's assets.[159] In Hegel's words, "The family as a legal person in relation to others must be represented by the husband as its head. In addition, he is primarily responsible for external acquisition and for caring for the family's needs, as well as for the control and administration of the family's resources" (PR §171). The father does not individually own the family's assets; he is only the family's representative in public contexts.[160] So it is through the father, the one who goes back and forth between the family and civil society, that the modern family emerges as an economic agent in its own right. It provides another indication that Hegel is aware of the extent to which the family relies on institutions beyond its borders in order to be able to accomplish its internal tasks.

Hegel stresses that a family's assets are a kind of property, but property that is jointly owned, a common property [*gemeinsames Eigentum*] (PR §171), which

---

[159] I don't want to exaggerate this point. As Landes rightly notes, Hegel thinks that all estates will involve the ownership of family property (p. 11) that can be inherited from one generation by another. The primary reason for thinking that Hegel has the bourgeois family in mind has to do with his views about the gendered division of labor.

[160] In "No Utopia," I discuss the male head's representational role in greater detail.

could sound like an oxymoron by Hegel's own lights. When Hegel first introduces the concept of property in his chapter on "Abstract Right," he rejects the very notion of collective ownership. He insists that communities cannot own property (except in exceptional circumstances administered by the state) because communities as communities do not have the same right to property that individuals as individuals do (PR §46A). In this way, Hegel establishes an intimate link between the concept of property and the concept of person. On the one hand, Hegel argues that person implies property, because realizing personal freedom requires property that is at your disposal to do with as you please. On the other hand, Hegel also argues that property implies person, because it is only persons that are the right sort of entities to own property.[161] Since Hegel is claiming that property is essentially private, it poses a challenge for the family. If Hegel wants to extend personhood to the family as a whole, he has to be able say that a family as family owns property. And if Hegel wants to regard the family as an entity whose members jointly own this property, he needs to be able to apply the concept of personhood to it.[162] So, it is the family's status as a person in its own right that grants individual members an automatic right to partake of the family's assets, to derive their fair share from it, as well as to inherit a part of it when the family naturally dissolves.

The male head has discretion over the family's collectively owned assets, which introduces problems that will need to be resolved. This is how Kimberly Hutchings puts it: "Although the head of the family does not own the family property as an individual, it is possible for him to treat that property as if he were an individual, to dissipate or accumulate, and to distribute it according to his own will and desires, like any other member of civil society."[163] In general, the state should not meddle in family relations, but when it comes to the administration of a family's assets, Hegel is willing to suspend this restriction. For example, Hegel urges the state to intervene when the male head is in the process of squandering the family's assets, leaving the other members without their fair share, especially the children without their rightful inheritance. Hegel's interest in the question of inheritance is perhaps unsurprising if we take his personal

---

[161] "Since my will, as personal and hence as the will of an individual [*des Einzelnen*], becomes objective in property, the latter takes on the character of *private property*; and common property, which may by its nature be owned by separate individuals, takes on the determination of an *inherently* [*an sich*] *dissolvable* community in which it is in itself [*für sich*] a matter for the arbitrary will whether or not I retain my share in it" (PR §46).

[162] I would go so far as to say that it is for this very reason that Hegel argues against a contractual conception of marriage. A married couple must constitute a single person not only because marriage shouldn't be marred by negotiations among self-interested individuals, but also because both parties, and eventually their offspring, becomes an entity that can own private property.

[163] Hutchings, "Living the Contradictions," p. 108.

situation into consideration. Before he landed a permanent academic position, Hegel relied on what he inherited upon his father's death in order to support himself as an unpaid lecturer.

Hegel is especially critical of the legal practice of drawing up a last will and testament, which gives the father the power to decide to whom to leave the family's assets. Such a legal practice would make it possible for a father to leave it to a friend.[164] It would also make it possible for a father to leave more of it to some children at the cost of others, for example, to sons rather than to daughters.[165] Hegel even criticizes laws that forbid a family's wealth from being divided into discrete parts, which would force members to remain bound to each other, making an exception only for situations in which a family's assets are an estate (*Majorat*) that cannot be neatly divided, in which case Hegel allows for the principle of progeniture. These highly concrete reflections on inheritance law seem at face value to violate Hegel's methodological commitment to refrain from dabbling in positive right and recommending which laws to put into place. But these reflections also indicate that Hegel is aware that patriarchy poses a threat to the family. While he is keen to keep this threat in check, he does not go so far as to criticize the family's patriarchal structure.

It is important to acknowledge that Hegel does not take property and assets or resources to be synonymous.[166] This is how Hegel distinguishes them:

> Not only does the family have property; as a universal and enduring person, it also incurs the need for possessions which are determined as permanent and secure, i.e. it needs resources. Abstract property contains the arbitrary moment of the particular need of the single individual [*das bloß Einzelnen*]; this is here transformed, along with the selfishness of desire, into care and acquisition of a *communal purpose*, i.e. into an *ethical quality*. (PR §170)

---

[164] This might suggest a return of blood as a criterion of family membership, but it does not in principle preclude that adopted children would be as entitled to a share in the family's inheritance.

[165] "That institution of the law of inheritance which, in order to *preserve* the *family* and to enhance its *renown* by means of *substitutions* and *family testamentary trusts*, either favors the sons by excluding the daughters from inheritance or favors the eldest son by excluding the remaining children (or allows any kind of inequality to arise) on the one hand infringes upon the freedom of property ... and on the other hand depends on an arbitrariness which in and for itself has no right to recognition" (PR §180R). This passage speaks against Hodge, who claims that the family's property belongs to the husband and that a wife has no legal recourse against him. In this context Hegel also makes clear that one should not place too much value on "this house" or "this kinship group." What matters is not the continuation of a specific blood line, but the perpetuation of the family as an institution.

[166] Okazaki, "Das Vermögen der Familie," traces the development of this concept across Hegel's lecture transcripts, showing that Hegel begins with *Familieneigentum* which eventually develops into *Familienvermögen*.

In this passage, Hegel alludes to assets *as resources*, since he makes clear that families need possessions in a way that exceeds individual needs. While private property is rooted in the single individual's right to do with things as he sees fit, material resources are rooted in the universal and enduring person, the family as a transgenerational entity that persists over time and that has a communal purpose.[167] It suggests that material resources introduce requirements, which Hegel describes as ethical, that are not already present in the concept of property.[168] Unlike private property, material resources are owned by a kind of community, though a community that is not an informal association, but that can be seen as universal and enduring in its own right. What a family as a family owns is not only private property, but also material resources. It would be to assume that "material resources" is simply another term (perhaps an ethically enriched term) for the very same thing as private property. As in the case of private property, these material resources would be owned by the family in a private manner, the line between who belongs to the family and so has a right to inheritance, and who does not belong to the family and so has no such right, sharply drawn.

But this is not Hegel's last word on the matter. In fact, he refers to material resources in a different context, in his subsequent chapter on "Civil Society." Hegel writes,

> In this dependence and reciprocity of work and the satisfaction of needs, *subjective selfishness* turns into a *contribution toward the satisfaction of the needs of everyone else*. By a dialectical movement, the particular is mediated by the universal so that each individual, in earning, producing, and enjoying on his own account, thereby earns and produces for the enjoyment of others. This necessity which is inherent in the interlinked dependence of each on all now appears to each individual in the form of *universal and permanent resources* (see §170) in which, through his education and skill, he has an opportunity to share; he is thereby assured of his livelihood, just as the universal resources are maintained and augmented by the income which he earns through his work. (PR §199)

In the context of the family, it seemed as if property and assets were two different ways of designating whatever a family privately own, belonging to family

---

[167] Mateo places emphasis on the transgenerational dimension of the family in virtue of which property turns into assets or resources. She brings out the irony of this relation when she writes: "Das Kind ermöglicht das Vermögen, insofern es die Person der Familie erst allgemein und fortdauernd macht."

[168] According to Ciavatta, Hegel's description of resources as *ethical* means that these resources consist not just of external things, but that they express intersubjective recognition. He provides the example of a family heirloom whose loss would feel like the loss of a part of oneself. See Ciavatta's discussion of family property pp. 173–189.

members only, even if to all of them equally. But in the context of civil society, it now looks as if property and assets refer to two different things, because these universal and permanent resources are not identical to that which is owned by a universal and permanent *person*, i.e. the family. Instead, we are told that these resources belong to everyone who contributes to their maintenance and augmentation by participating in the system of needs and its division of labor. The key here is to see that the model of the family will be insufficient for capturing the significance of assets in this second context. These resources are universal not because they belong to all members of a family, but because they belong to all members of civil society. And these resources are permanent not because the offspring of certain parents benefit from them, but because they constitute a reservoir on which everyone relies and from which everyone draws. I am inclined to call them *communal resources*. If we think through what they are and why they enable or empower the realization of freedom, we will be compelled to move beyond the borders of the private family and its private property, and to realize that it is in this larger space of common work and common need where they truly reside.

As I read him, Hegel is placing the concept of material resources front and center because he thinks that everyone needs them in order to develop into singular individuals and in order to contribute to the development of others, first and foremost children. It is Hegel's way of capturing the simple idea – an idea that the parents who are busy hoarding and transmitting their wealth would be the last to deny – that freedom presupposes recourse to material resources. This passage can be interpreted as Hegel's version of Adam Smith's "invisible hand" governing the market and ensuring that even though each individual is producing only for his own enjoyment and the enjoyment of his family, he inadvertently produces for the enjoyment of everyone else. But the same passage can also be interpreted in a different spirit, as anticipating Karl Marx's principle "from each according to his abilities, to each according to his needs."[169] This would forge another path that leads away from the family form, since it would suggest that our basic needs might be better accommodated in other contexts, than that of the family. But Hegel does not tell us how to sketch such an alternative. He seems to share Marx's own conviction that it is not his job to write recipes for the kitchens of the future.

5 Conclusion

If we follow Hegel's line of defense of the family as an institution to this point, we can draw two general conclusions about the family form on his behalf. The first is that singular individuality, ethical love, and material resources are

---

[169] M.E. Obrien mentions this principle in relation of family abolition on p. 194.

necessary for the realization of freedom as being by oneself in another. This strikes me as a significant upshot of Hegel's defense of the family. Although those invested in the project of abolishing the family could circumvent Hegel's views on the family, I hoped to show that Hegel offers ways of specifying the goods that are presumably worth preserving, and of understanding how these goods became knowable and how they are intertwined through participation in families. According to Hegel, the family is a rational institution to the extent to which it fosters the development of singular individuality and provides a context for its continued recognition. For this reason, singular individuality can only be realized in conjunction with ethical love and with material resources. If we want to keep the baby of the family but get rid of its institutional bathwater, it would be useful to see this baby not simply as a list of good things about families, but as a whole whose parts are intimately related.

The second is that even though it is within the family that singular individuality, ethical love, and material resources have been discovered and developed, these need not belong exclusively to the family, and even more narrowly, to the modern nuclear family. As the example of material resources demonstrates, Hegel's account of the family is not ruling out transforming the family so radically that it bears virtually no resemblance to our current institution, because the family could very well lose its form as a privatized source of primary care for its members. Whether we want to call this a case of family abolition or family reform will depend on what the concept of the family turns out to be, and on whether the family as a concept needs to be refurbished or abandoned. Hegel's account of the family can also serve as a source of caution: since the family is not and never was self-enclosed and self-sufficient, it cannot be radically transformed without a substantial reorganization of our material lives, and more generally of ethical life. When all is said and done, there might be many more obstacles that stand in the way of finding out what lies on the other side. My goal has been to convince you that Hegel's idea of the family is not one of them.

Bibliography

Primary

Elements of the Philosophy of Right (trans. H. B. Nisbet), Cambridge University Press, 1991.
Grundlinien der Philosophy des Rechts, Suhrkamp, 1986.
Lectures of the Philosophy of World History (trans. Nisbet), Cambridge, 1981.
Phenomenology of Spirit (trans. Miller), Oxford, 1977.
Phänomenologie des Geistes, Suhrkamp, 1986.
Encyclopedia of the Philosophical Sciences Volumes I and II, Claredon Press, 2004.
The Science of Logic (trans. Di Giovanni), Cambridge, 2015.

Secondary

Beauvoir, Simone. *The Second Sex*. New York: Vintage Books, 1949.
Benhabib, Seyla. "On Hegel, Woman, and Irony," in *Situating the Self: Gender, Community, and Post-Modernism in Contemporary Ethics*. New York: Routledge 1992, 242–259.
Berg, Anastasia and Rachel Wiseman. *What Are Children For? On Ambivalence and Choice*. New York: St. Martin's Press, 2024.
Bockenheimer, Eva. *Hegels Familien- und Geschlechtertheorie*. Hamburg: Felix Meiner Verlag, 2013.
Brake, Elizabeth. "Love's Paradox: Making Sense of Hegel on Marriage," *Women's Philosophy Review*, 22, 1999, 80–104.
  Minimizing Marriage: Marriage, Morality and the Law. Oxford: Oxford University Press, 2012.
Brauer, Susanne. *Natur und Sittlichkeit: Die Familie in Hegels Rechtsphilosophie*. Baden-Baden: Karl Alber, 2007.
Butler, Judith. *Antigone's Claim: Kinship Between Life and Death*. New York: Columbia University Press, 2002.
Cavell, Stanley. *Pursuits of Happiness: the Hollywood Comedy of Remarriage*. Cambridge, MA: Harvard University Press, 1984.
Ciavatta, David V. *Spirit, the Family, and the Unconscious in Hegel's Philosophy*, Albany: SUNY Press, 2009.
Cusk, Rachel. *A Life's Work: On Becoming a Mother*. New York: Picador, 2001.
Daub, Adrian. *Uncivil Unions: The Metaphysics of Marriage in German Idealism and Romanticism*. Chicago: University of Chicago Press, 2012.
Davis, Angela Y. *Women, Race & Class*. London: Penguin, 1981.

De Boer, Karin. "Hegel's Antigone and the Dialectics of Cultural Difference," *Philosophy Today* 47:5, 2003, 140–146.

Deranty, Jean-Philippe. "The 'Son of Civil Society': Tensions in Hegel's Account of Womanhood," *Philosophical Forum*, 31:2, 2000, 145–162.

Easton, Susan M. "Hegel and Feminism," in David Lamb (ed.), *Hegel and Modern Philosophy*. New York: Croom Helm, 1987, 30–55.

Elshtain, Jean. *Public Man, Private Woman: Women in Social and Political Thought*. Princeton, NJ: Princeton University Press, 1981.

Fisher, Mark. *Capitalist Realism: Is There No Alternative?* Winchester: Zero Books, 2009.

Geller, Jay. "Hegel's Self-Conscious Woman," *Modern Language Quarterly*, 53:2, 1992, 173–199.

Gregoratto, Federica. *Love Troubles: A Philosophy of Eros*. New York: Columbia University Press, 2025.

Halper, Edward C. "Hegel's Family Values," *The Review of Metaphysics*, 54:4, 2001, 815–858.

Hausen, Karin. "Die Polarisierung der 'Geschlechtscharaktere' – Eine Spiegelung der Dissoziation von Erwerbs- und Familienleben," in Werner Conze (ed.), *Sozialgeschichte der Familie in der Neuzeit Europas*, 1978, 363–393.

Heim, Léon A. "'Natürlicher sittlicher Geist': Die Familie als sittliches Naturverhältnis," in *Hegel-Jahrbuch*. Berlin: Duncker & Humblot, forthcoming.

Heisenberg, Thimo. "Hegel on Childless Marriage," *Hegel Bulletin,* forthcoming.

Hodge, Joanna. "Women and the Hegelian State," in Ellen Kennedy and Susan Mendus (eds.), *Women and Western Political Philosophy: Kant to Nietzsche*. London: St. Martin's Press, 1987, 127–158.

Honneth, Axel. *The Struggle for Recognition: The Moral Grammar of Social Conflicts*. Cambridge, MA: MIT Press, 1995.

Freedom's Right: The Social Foundations of Democratic Life. New York: Columbia University Press, 2015.

Hopwood, Mark. "The Extremely Difficult Realization That Something Other Than Oneself Is Real: Iris Murdoch and Love and Moral Agency," *European Journal of Philosophy*, 26:1, 2018, 477–501.

Hutchings, Kimberly. *Hegel and Feminist Philosophy*, Cambridge: Polity Press, 2003.

Hutchings, Kimberly and Tuija Pulkkinen (eds.), *Hegel's Philosophy and Feminist Thought: Beyond Antigone?* New York: Palgrave Macmillan, 2010.

Irigaray, Luce. *Speculum of the Other Woman*. Ithaca, NY: Cornell University Press, 1985.

Irigaray, Luce. "Eternal Irony of the Community" in Patricia J. Mills (ed.), *Feminist Interpretations of G. W. F. Hegel*, University Park, PA: Penn State University Press, 1996, 45–57.

Jacobs, Carol. "Dusting Antigone," *MLN*, 111:5, 1996, 889–917.

Jaeggi, Rahel. *Critique of Forms of Life*. Cambridge, MA: Harvard University Press, 2018.

Kain, Philip J. "Hegel, Recognition, and Same-Sex Marriage," *Journal of Social Philosophy*, 46:2, 2015, 226–241.

Katz, Gal. "'Love Is Only between Living Beings Who are Equal in Power': On What Is Alive (And What Is Dead) in Hegel's Account of Marriage," *European Journal of Philosophy*, 28:1, 2020, 93–109.

Kobe, Zdravko. "Keine Frau muss müssen? Hegel in the Time of MeToo," *Crisis and Critique* 8:2, 2021, 206–225.

Kolodny, Niko. "Love as Valuing a Relationship," *The Philosophical Review* 112:2, 2003, 135–189.

Krell, David Farrell. "Lucinde's Shame: Hegel, Sensuous Woman, and the Law," in Patricia J. Mills (ed.), *Feminist Interpretations of G. W. F. Hegel*, University Park, PA: Penn State University Press, 1996, 89–107.

Landes, Joan. "Hegel's Conception of the Family," *Polity*, 14:1, 1981, 5–28.

Lettow, Susanne. "Re-articulating Genealogy: Hegel on Kinship, Race and Reproduction," *Hegel Bulletin* 42:2, 2021, 256–276.

Lewis, Sophie. *Abolish the Family: A Manifesto for Care and Liberation*. London: Verso, 2022.

Locatelli, Silvia. "Hegel's Antigone: A Revolutionary Role," Unpublished Manuscript.

Loyd, Genevieve. "Feminism in History of Philosophy: Appropriating the Past," in M. Fricker and Jennifer. Hornsby (eds.), *Cambridge Companion to Feminism in Philosophy*. Cambridge: Cambridge University Press, 2000, 245–263.

Mateo, Marina Martinez. *Kritik der Familie*, Unpublished Manuscript.

May, Simon. *Love: A New Understanding of an Ancient Emotion*. Oxford: Oxford University Press, 2019.

Moland, Lydia. *Hegel's Aesthetics: The Art of Idealism*. Oxford: Oxford University Press, 2019.

Moyar, Dean. *Hegel's Value: Justice as the Living Good*. Oxford: Oxford University Press, 2021.

Munoz-Dardé, Véronique. "Is the Family to be Abolished Then?" *Proceedings of the Aristotelian Society*, 99, 1999, 37–56.

Mills, Patricia J. "Hegel's Antigone," in Patricia J. Mills (ed.), *Feminist Interpretations of G. W. Hegel*, University Park, PA: Penn State University Press, 1996, 59–88.

ed. *Feminist Interpretations of G. W. F. Hegel*. University Park: Penn State University Press, 1996.

Murdoch, Iris. "The Sublime and the Good," in Peter Conradi (ed.), *Existentialists and Mystics: Writings on Philosophy and Literature*. New York: Penguin Books, 1999. 205–220.

Neuhouser, Frederick. *Foundations of Hegel's Social Theory: Actualizing Freedom*. Cambridge, MA: Harvard University Press, 2000.

Diagnosing Social Pathology: Rousseau, Hegel, Marx and Durkheim. Cambridge: Cambridge University Press, 2023.

Novakovic, Andreja. *Hegel on Second Nature in Ethical Life*. Cambridge: Cambridge University Press, 2017.

"No Utopia: Hegel on the Gendered Division of Labor," in Dean Moyar, Kate Padgett Walsh, and Sebastian Rand (eds.), *Hegel's Philosophy of Right: Critical Perspectives on Freedom and History*. London: Routledge, 2023, 206–232.

Novakovic, Andreja and Oksana Maksymchuk. "Hegel and Plato on How to Become Good," *British Journal for the History of Philosophy*, 30:4, 2022, 707–726.

O'Brian, M. E. *Family Abolition: Capitalism and the Communizing of Care*. London: Pluto Press, 2023.

O'Brien, Mary. "Hegel: Man, Physiology, Fate," in Patricia J. Mills (ed.), *Feminist Interpretations of G. W. F. Hegel*, University Park, PA: Penn State University Press, 1996, 177–207.

Okazaki, Yuka. "Das Vermögen der Familie in Hegels Rechtsphilosophie," *Hegel-Jahrbuch* 2019:1, 2019, 646–652.

Olsen, Frances. "Hegel, Sexual Ethics, and the Oppression of Women: Comments on Krell's 'Lucinde's Shame'," in Patricia J. Mills (ed.), *Feminist Interpretations of G.W.F. Hegel*, University Park, PA: Penn State University Press, 1996, 109–117.

Pateman, Carole "Hegel, Marriage, and the Standpoint of Contract," in Patricia J. Mills (ed.), *Feminist Interpretations of G. W. F. Hegel*, University Park, PA: Penn State University Press, 1996, 209–223.

The Sexual Contract, Stanford, CA: Stanford University Press, 1988.

Paul, L. A. *Transformative Experience*. Oxford University Press, 2016.

Pinkard, Terry. *Hegel's Phenomenology: The Sociality of Reason*. Cambridge: Cambridge University Press, 1996.

Ravven, Heidi. "Has Hegel Anything to Say to Feminists?" *The Owl of Minerva*, 19:2, 1988, 149–168.

Rawls, John. *A Theory of Justice*. Cambridge, MA: Harvard University Press.

Rodgers, Dorothy. *America's First Women Philosophers: Transplanting Hegel, 1860 – 1925*. London: Continuum, 2005.

Rosa, Sophie K. *Radical Intimacy*, London: Pluto Press, 2022.

Scholz, Sally J. "Reproductive Labor: The Impact of the Patriarchal Family on Hegel's Phenomenology," *Clio*, 22:4, 1993.

Spillers, Hortense. "Mama's Baby, Papa's Maybe: An American Grammar Book," *Diacritics*, 17:2, 1987, 64–81.

Stafford, Antoinette. "The Feminist Critique of Hegel on Women and the Family," *Animus*, 2, 1997, 64–92.

Steiner, George. *Antigones*. New Haven: Yale University Press, 1984.

Stone, Alison. "Gender, the Family, and the Organic State," in Thom Brooks (ed.), *Hegel's Philosophy of Right: Essays on Ethics, Politics, and Law*, Hoboken, NJ: Wiley-Blackwell,. 2012, 143–164.

"Hegel on law, women, and contract," in Maria Drakopoulou (ed.), *Feminist Encounters with Legal Philosophy*. New York: Routledge 2014, 104–122.

Tzelepis, Elena. "Antigone's Dissidence," in Susanne Lettow and Tuija Pulkkinen (eds.), *Palgrave Handbook of German Idealism and Feminist Philosophy*, London: Palgrave Macmillan, 2022, 249–270.

Vernon, Jim. "Free Love: A Hegelian Defense of Same-Sex Marriage Rights," *The Southern Journal of Philosophy* 47:1, 2010, 69–89.

Vuillerod, Jean-Baptiste. *Hegel Féministe: Les Aventures D'Antigone*. Paris: Vrin, 2020.

Willett, Cynthia. "Hegel, Antigone, and the Possibility of Ecstatic Dialogue," *Philosophy and Literature* 14:2, 1990, 268–283.

Wood, Allen. *Hegel's Ethical Thought*, Cambridge: Cambridge University Press, 1990.

Zizek in "Hegel on Marriage," *E-Flux Journal*, 24, 2012, 1–10. www.e-flux.com/journal/34/68365/hegel-on-marriage/.

Cambridge Elements ≡

The Philosophy of Georg Wilhelm Friedrich Hegel

Sebastian Stein
Heidelberg University

Sebastian Stein is a Research Associate at Heidelberg University. He is co-editor of *Hegel's Political Philosophy* (2017), *Hegel and Contemporary Practical Philosophy* (with James Gledhill, 2019) and *Hegel's Encyclopedic System* (2021), and has authored several journal articles and chapters on Aristotle, Kant, post-Kantian idealism, and (neo-)naturalism.

Joshua Wretzel
Pennsylvania State University

Joshua Wretzel is Assistant Teaching Professor of Philosophy at the Pennsylvania State University. He is the co-editor of *Hegel's Encyclopedic System* and *Hegel's Encyclopedia of the Philosophical Sciences: A Critical Guide* (Cambridge). His articles on Hegel and the German philosophical tradition have appeared in multiple edited collections and peer-reviewed journals, including the *European Journal of Philosophy* and *International Journal for Philosophical Studies*.

About the Series

These Elements provide insights into all aspects of Hegel's thought and its relationship to philosophical currents before, during, and after his time. They offer fresh perspectives on well-established topics in Hegel studies, and in some cases use Hegelian categories to define new research programs and to complement existing discussions.

Cambridge Elements⁼

The Philosophy of Georg Wilhelm Friedrich Hegel

Elements in the Series

Hegel and Heidegger on Time
Ioannis Trisokkas

Hegel and Colonialism
Daniel James and Franz Knappik

Hegel's Sublation of Transcendental Idealism
Christian Krijnen

Hegel's Philosophy of Nature
Christian Martin

Hegel on the Family Form
Andreja Novakovic

A full series listing is available at: www.cambridge.org/EPGH

For EU product safety concerns, contact us at Calle de José Abascal, 56–1°, 28003 Madrid, Spain or eugpsr@cambridge.org.

www.ingramcontent.com/pod-product-compliance
Lightning Source LLC
LaVergne TN
LVHW011857060526
838200LV00054B/4394